Clarity and Growth

Unlocking Your Best Life

Eva Binder

Clarity and Growth 1

Unlocking Your Best Life 1

Eva Binder 1

Chapter 1: Foundations of Self Awareness 5

The Mirror of Self Reflection 5

Breaking Through Mental Fog 8

Identifying Core Values 11

Mapping Your Current Reality 15

Establishing Your True North 18

Chapter 2: Clearing the Path... 22

Recognizing Limiting Beliefs.. 22

Understanding Emotional Patterns 25

Releasing Past Narratives 29

Reframing Your Story 32

Building Mental Clarity Practices 35

Creating Space for Growth 39

Designing Your Environment for Success 42

Chapter 3: The Architecture of Personal Growth 46

Understanding Growth Mindset 46

The Science of Habit Formation 49

Building Resilience 52

Mastering Emotional Intelligence...................................56

Developing Strategic Thinking..59

Chapter 4: Actionable Clarity Tools................................... 63

Decision Making Frameworks.. 63

Priority Alignment Systems.. 66

Goal Setting Mastery.. 69

Chapter 5: Growth Acceleration Strategies 73

High Performance Habits..73

Strategic Learning Methods 76

Personal Innovation Practices.....................................79

Energy Management.. 82

Time Mastery... 85

Chapter 6: Integration and Implementation 88

Creating Your Growth Blueprint............................. 88

Building Support Systems 90

Measuring Progress 93

Adapting to Change..95

Chapter 7: Sustaining Long Term Success 98

The Continuity Framework 98

Evolution of Goals.. 100

Legacy Building..102

Mentoring Others...105

Living Your Best Life...107

Chapter 1: Foundations of Self Awareness

The Mirror of Self Reflection

Self-reflection begins in stillness, in those quiet moments when we dare to look deeply into our own consciousness. Like a mirror that reveals both surface features and hidden depths, genuine self-reflection illuminates aspects of ourselves we may have overlooked or chosen to ignore. The practice requires more than casual introspection – it demands courage, honesty, and a willingness to examine both our proudest achievements and our deepest struggles.

Consider the metaphor of a lake at dawn. When the water is perfectly still, it reflects everything with pristine clarity: the surrounding trees, the sky above, even the subtle interplay of light and shadow. Similarly, our minds must achieve a state of calm receptivity to reflect our true nature accurately. Yet just as a gentle breeze can disturb the lake's surface, our thoughts and emotions often create ripples that distort our self-perception.

The art of self-reflection extends beyond mere self-examination. It requires developing the capacity to observe our thoughts, feelings, and behaviors with the detachment of a curious scientist and the compassion of a dear friend. This dual perspective allows us to acknowledge our imperfections without harsh judgment while maintaining the objectivity necessary for genuine insight.

Time spent in self-reflection yields profound benefits. Research has shown that regular introspective practice enhances emotional intelligence, improves decision-making capabilities, and strengthens interpersonal relationships. Yet many avoid looking too deeply within, fearing what they might discover. This fear, while natural, often prevents us from accessing the very insights that could catalyze our growth.

Effective self-reflection begins with creating the right environment – both external and internal. Find a quiet space where interruptions are unlikely. Some prefer the solitude of early morning, others the contemplative quiet of evening. The specific time matters less than the consistency of practice. Settle into a comfortable position, allowing your body to relax while maintaining mental alertness.

As you begin this practice, notice the tendency of your mind to wander or to shy away from certain thoughts. This resistance itself offers valuable information about areas that might benefit from closer examination. Start with gentle questions: What emotions have I experienced today? What triggered these feelings? What patterns emerge when I examine my responses to various situations?

Journaling serves as a powerful tool for deepening self-reflection. The act of writing transforms abstract thoughts into concrete observations, allowing us to examine our experiences from new angles. Through written exploration, we often discover connections and patterns that remained hidden in mere mental reflection.

Beyond individual practice, feedback from trusted others can enhance our self-reflection. Like additional mirrors offering different angles of view, the perspectives of those who know us well can illuminate blind spots in our self-perception. However, discernment is crucial – we must balance external input with our own inner knowing.

The practice of self-reflection reveals not only areas for improvement but also sources of strength and resilience we may have overlooked. It uncovers the values that truly guide us, not merely those we claim to hold. This clarity becomes invaluable when facing difficult decisions or navigating challenging transitions.

Regular self-reflection also develops our capacity for presence. As we become more attuned to our inner landscape, we naturally become more aware of our immediate experience. This heightened awareness allows us to respond to life's challenges with greater wisdom and less reactivity.

Perhaps most importantly, self-reflection nurtures self-compassion. As we observe our thoughts and behaviors with gentle curiosity rather than harsh judgment, we develop a more nuanced and accepting relationship with ourselves. This compassionate self-awareness creates a foundation for authentic growth and meaningful change.

The mirror of self-reflection reveals both what is and what could be. It shows us not only our current reality but also glimpses of our potential. Through this practice, we begin to recognize the gap between who we are and who we aspire to become. This recognition, far from being discouraging, provides the clarity necessary for intentional growth.

Breaking Through Mental Fog

Mental fog descends like a heavy veil, obscuring our thoughts and dulling our cognitive edge. This cognitive haze manifests in countless ways - forgotten appointments, misplaced keys, difficulty concentrating, or that frustrating sensation of thoughts hovering just beyond reach. Yet beneath this temporary cloudiness lies our natural mental clarity, waiting to emerge.

Understanding the root causes of mental fog empowers us to navigate through it effectively. Sleep deprivation, chronic stress, poor nutrition, and information overload frequently contribute to this state of mental murkiness. The modern lifestyle, with its constant digital stimulation and relentless pace, creates perfect conditions for cognitive overwhelm. Research indicates that the average person processes more information in a single day than their ancestors encountered in a month.

The path through mental fog begins with recognition. Notice the subtle signs: increased forgetfulness, difficulty making decisions, reduced emotional regulation, or a general sense of disconnection from your usual mental acuity. These symptoms often appear gradually, making them easy to dismiss until they significantly impact your performance and wellbeing.

Physical movement serves as a powerful antidote to mental stagnation. When fog settles in, engaging in deliberate physical activity - even a brief walk - stimulates blood flow to the brain and triggers the release of clarity-enhancing neurochemicals. Studies consistently show that regular exercise improves cognitive function, enhances memory, and reduces mental fatigue.

Nutritional choices profoundly influence mental clarity. The brain consumes approximately twenty percent of the body's energy resources, requiring high-quality fuel to function optimally. Hydration plays an equally crucial role - even mild dehydration can impair cognitive performance and mood. Complex carbohydrates, healthy fats, and proteins provide sustained mental energy, while excessive sugar and processed foods can contribute to cognitive fluctuations.

Strategic rest proves essential for breaking through mental fog. This doesn't necessarily mean sleeping more, though quality sleep remains fundamental. Instead, incorporate deliberate breaks throughout your day - moments of mental stillness that allow your brain to process information and reset. The technique of time-blocking, alternating focused work periods with brief restorative breaks, helps maintain mental clarity over extended periods.

Environmental factors significantly impact cognitive function. Cluttered spaces often reflect and reinforce mental chaos. Creating an organized, minimalist workspace reduces cognitive load and helps maintain mental clarity. Natural light exposure regulates circadian rhythms, while proper ventilation ensures optimal oxygen levels for brain function. Consider the subtle ways your environment might be contributing to mental fog.

Digital overwhelm frequently underlies cognitive cloudiness. The constant ping of notifications, endless scroll of social media, and pressure to remain continuously connected fragment attention and exhaust mental resources. Implementing digital boundaries - designated offline periods, notification controls, and structured information consumption - helps restore mental clarity.

Mindfulness practices offer powerful tools for dispersing mental fog. Regular meditation strengthens attention, improves emotional regulation, and enhances cognitive flexibility. Simple breathing exercises can quickly shift your mental state, providing immediate relief from cognitive overwhelm. These practices build resilience against future mental fog by strengthening your ability to maintain focus and clarity under pressure.

Writing serves as both diagnostic tool and treatment for mental fog. Journaling helps externalize cluttered thoughts, revealing patterns and providing clarity. The act of writing engages different neural pathways than typing, potentially offering unique benefits for cognitive processing. Through regular writing practice, you develop greater awareness of your mental states and more effective strategies for maintaining clarity.

Social connection plays an unexpected role in mental clarity. Engaging in meaningful conversation stimulates cognitive function and provides fresh perspectives that can help cut through mental fog. However, choose these interactions wisely - not all social engagement proves equally beneficial for mental clarity.

The journey through mental fog requires patience and persistence. Quick fixes rarely provide lasting solutions. Instead, focus on building a comprehensive approach that addresses physical, mental, and environmental factors. Track your progress, noting which strategies prove most effective for your unique situation. This personalized understanding becomes invaluable for preventing and addressing future episodes of mental fog.

Identifying Core Values

Core values serve as the internal compass that guides our decisions, shapes our behavior, and defines our character. They represent our deepest convictions about what matters most, transcending fleeting emotions or circumstantial pressures. Like foundational pillars supporting a magnificent structure, these values provide stability and direction throughout life's journey.

Consider Sarah, a successful executive who found herself increasingly disconnected from her work despite her achievements. Through careful self-examination, she discovered that creativity and autonomy ranked among her highest values, yet her role emphasized conformity and rigid procedures. This misalignment explained her growing dissatisfaction and ultimately guided her toward a more fulfilling career path that honored her core values.

The process of identifying core values requires diving beneath surface-level preferences to explore the fundamental principles that truly motivate us. While external influences – family, culture, society – shape our initial value system, authentic core values emerge from personal experience and deep reflection. They reveal themselves in moments of decisive action, when faced with difficult choices, or during times of significant challenge.

Values often announce their presence through emotional resonance. Pay attention to situations that provoke strong feelings – both positive and negative. When you feel most alive, engaged, and authentic, you're likely operating in alignment with your core values. Conversely, experiences that trigger persistent discomfort or resistance may signal a values violation.

Research in positive psychology suggests that people who live in accordance with their core values demonstrate greater resilience, higher life satisfaction, and more meaningful relationships. These individuals navigate challenges with clearer purpose and recover more quickly from setbacks. Their decisions, guided by well-understood values, tend to yield more satisfying long-term outcomes.

Historical figures who achieved remarkable impact often demonstrated unwavering commitment to their core values. Consider Nelson Mandela's dedication to equality and reconciliation, or Marie Curie's pursuit of scientific truth. Their values provided direction through tremendous adversity and ultimately shaped their enduring legacies.

The identification of core values requires both reflection and action. Start by examining peak experiences – moments when you felt most fulfilled or proud. What principles were you honoring in those instances? Review your heroes and role models. What qualities do you admire in them? These answers offer clues to your own core values.

Writing plays a crucial role in this discovery process. Document your reactions to daily events, noting when you feel most aligned or disturbed. Patterns will emerge, revealing the values that consistently influence your responses. This written record becomes invaluable as you refine your understanding of your fundamental principles.

Many mistake preferences or aspirations for core values. A preference for order differs from a core value of integrity. An aspiration for wealth differs from a core value of security. True core values remain constant across contexts and time, while preferences and aspirations may shift with circumstances.

Some values may conflict with each other, requiring careful prioritization. A value of adventure might occasionally tension with a value of responsibility. Understanding your hierarchy of values helps navigate these conflicts with greater wisdom and less internal struggle.

Physical environment often reflects and reinforces core values. Someone who values learning might surround themselves with books and educational opportunities. One who values connection might create spaces conducive to gathering and conversation. Aligning your environment with your values strengthens their influence on daily life.

Relationships flourish when built on shared or complementary values. Understanding your core values improves partner selection, strengthens existing bonds, and helps resolve conflicts through reference to common principles. It also allows for more authentic self-expression and deeper connections.

Professional satisfaction correlates strongly with value alignment. Organizations increasingly recognize that employees perform best when their personal values align with company culture. Understanding your core values enables more informed career choices and stronger workplace relationships.

As life evolves, our understanding of our values may deepen, though the values themselves remain relatively stable. Regular reflection helps refine this understanding, ensuring decisions continue to align with our fundamental principles. This ongoing process of value clarification contributes to personal growth and life satisfaction.

The power of identified core values lies in their application. They serve as decision-making criteria, conflict resolution tools, and sources of motivation. When faced with difficult choices, referring to your core values often illuminates the optimal path forward. They provide clarity in confusion and courage in adversity.

Mapping Your Current Reality

The journey of personal transformation begins with an unflinching assessment of where you stand today. Like a cartographer mapping uncharted territory, you must survey your current landscape with precision and honesty, noting both the peaks of achievement and valleys of challenge that shape your present circumstances.

Picture yourself as an artist stepping back from a canvas, observing the interplay of colors and shapes that comprise your life's current composition. Every brushstroke - your relationships, career, health, finances, emotional well-being - contributes to this complex portrait of your present reality. Understanding these elements in their totality provides the foundation for meaningful change.

The process of mapping requires methodical observation across multiple dimensions. Begin with your daily rhythms - the patterns that structure your time and energy. Notice how your mornings unfold, the ebb and flow of your productivity, the quality of your rest. These patterns reveal much about your current priorities and challenges.

Consider David, a marketing executive who believed lack of time prevented him from pursuing his passion for writing. Through careful reality mapping, he discovered he spent three hours daily on social media and streaming services. This revelation transformed his perception of his available resources and led to a dramatic restructuring of his daily schedule.

Your emotional landscape demands equal attention. Track your predominant moods, emotional triggers, and recurring thoughts. Notice which situations energize you and which drain your reserves. These emotional patterns often illuminate deeper truths about your current state of being and areas ripe for growth.

Professional reality encompasses more than your job title or income. Examine your level of engagement, the alignment between your work and values, your relationships with colleagues, and your trajectory within your field. Map both the tangible metrics of success and the intangible elements of satisfaction and purpose.

Relationships form another crucial layer of your current reality. Beyond simply listing important connections, assess the quality and depth of these bonds. Note patterns in your interactions, areas of support and strain, and the overall balance between giving and receiving in your relationships. This relational mapping often reveals surprising insights about your social patterns and needs.

Financial reality requires particular objectivity. Document not just numbers but your relationship with money - your spending patterns, saving habits, financial fears, and aspirations. Understanding your current financial position, including both assets and liabilities, provides crucial context for future planning.

Physical well-being contributes fundamentally to your current reality. Map your energy levels, sleep quality, exercise habits, and nutritional patterns. Note any persistent health concerns or physical limitations that impact your daily life. This bodily awareness grounds your understanding in tangible, measurable aspects of your present state.

Your environmental reality - the spaces where you live and work - shapes your experience in subtle but significant ways. Observe how your surroundings support or hinder your goals. Consider the organization, aesthetics, and functionality of these spaces. Your environment often reflects and reinforces your internal state.

Time management reveals much about your current reality. Track how you actually spend your hours, not just how you think you spend them. This temporal mapping often uncovers surprising disparities between perceived and actual time allocation, highlighting opportunities for realignment.

Knowledge and skills constitute another vital dimension of your present landscape. Catalog your expertise, identifying both strengths and gaps in your capabilities. This inventory helps identify areas where additional learning or development might advance your goals.

Spiritual or philosophical reality - your sense of meaning, purpose, and connection to something larger than yourself - adds depth to your current reality map. Examine your beliefs, values in action, and sources of inspiration or guidance.

Creating this comprehensive map requires both courage and compassion. You must maintain the objectivity to see things as they are while avoiding harsh self-judgment. Remember, this mapping process serves not to criticize but to illuminate your starting point for growth.

Document your observations with specificity and nuance. Like a detailed topographical map, your reality map should note both major landmarks and subtle variations in terrain. This detailed understanding enables more strategic and effective planning for future growth.

The resulting map becomes a powerful tool for decision-making and goal-setting. It provides context for your aspirations, helping you identify which changes might yield the most significant impact. Your current reality map serves as both compass and foundation for the transformative journey ahead.

Establishing Your True North

Your True North exists beyond the magnetic pull of external expectations and societal pressures, standing as an unwavering beacon that guides life's most consequential decisions. Like the celestial pole star that ancient mariners used to navigate vast oceans, this internal compass provides direction through life's turbulent waters and moments of profound choice.

Consider the story of Maria, a gifted surgeon who appeared to embody success by every conventional measure. Her prestigious position, considerable income, and professional accolades suggested fulfillment, yet a persistent inner whisper spoke of misalignment. Through deep introspection, she discovered her True North lay not in performing surgeries but in revolutionizing medical education. This realization, though daunting, illuminated her authentic path forward.

The process of establishing your True North demands excavating beneath layers of accumulated expectations, cultural conditioning, and inherited beliefs. These external influences, while formative, often obscure our deepest truths. Like an archaeologist carefully brushing away sediment to reveal ancient artifacts, we must gently clear away these overlying layers to uncover our authentic direction.

True North manifests in moments of perfect clarity - those rare instances when action flows from pure conviction rather than obligation or fear. These moments often arise unexpectedly: in the quiet of early morning reflection, during passionate conversation with a trusted friend, or amid the focused flow of meaningful work. They offer glimpses of our most authentic selves, unencumbered by doubt or external pressure.

Research in positive psychology reveals that individuals who align their lives with their internal compass report significantly higher levels of life satisfaction and resilience. This alignment creates a sense of congruence between internal values and external actions, reducing the psychological friction that arises from living counter to our deepest truths.

The establishment of True North requires careful attention to internal signals. Notice what energizes rather than depletes, what generates excitement rather than obligation, what feels expansive rather than constrictive. These subtle indicators often point toward your authentic direction, even when that direction challenges conventional wisdom or comfortable patterns.

Legacy considerations often clarify True North orientation. Imagine yourself at life's end, reflecting back on your journey. What achievements would fill you with genuine pride? What contributions would feel most meaningful? These future-focused reflections often cut through present-day noise to reveal your essential direction.

Physical sensations provide valuable guidance in this discovery process. The body often signals alignment or discord before the conscious mind recognizes it. A sense of lightness, expansiveness, or quiet excitement frequently accompanies True North-aligned choices, while heaviness, constriction, or anxiety often signals deviation from your authentic path.

Relationships play a crucial role in True North navigation. Notice which connections inspire you to grow versus those that encourage stagnation. Authentic direction often becomes clearer in the presence of those who support our highest expression rather than those who reinforce limiting patterns.

Written reflection serves as a powerful tool for establishing True North. Regular journaling, especially during periods of transition or decision-making, helps identify patterns and themes that point toward your authentic direction. These written records become invaluable reference points during times of uncertainty or doubt.

Environmental factors influence our ability to discern True North. Creating spaces for quiet reflection, surrounding yourself with inspiring elements, and minimizing distractions enhance your capacity to hear your internal guidance. This physical organization supports the mental clarity necessary for authentic direction-finding.

The process requires patience and persistence. True North reveals itself gradually, through consistent attention and willing adjustment. Like a pilot making constant small corrections to stay on course, establishing your authentic direction involves ongoing calibration and refinement.

Financial considerations often create apparent conflicts with True North orientation. Yet creative solutions frequently emerge when we remain committed to authentic direction while acknowledging practical realities. The path forward may require stepping stones rather than immediate leaps, but maintaining clear orientation ensures progress toward genuine fulfillment.

Your True North, once established, becomes both anchor and compass. It provides stability during storms of uncertainty while pointing the way toward your next evolution. This internal guidance system, refined through experience and reflection, enables decisions that honor both present circumstances and future aspirations, creating a life of meaningful progression rather than mere motion.

Chapter 2: Clearing the Path

Recognizing Limiting Beliefs

Limiting beliefs operate like invisible prison walls, constructed from past experiences, cultural conditioning, and misinterpreted failures. These subtle yet powerful constraints shape our perception of what's possible, often without our conscious awareness. They whisper narratives of inadequacy, impossibility, and unworthiness, creating boundaries that exist primarily in our minds.

Picture Emma, a talented writer who carried the belief that "creative success requires extraordinary talent." This seemingly innocuous thought pattern led her to abandon countless manuscripts before completion. Only when she recognized this belief as a self-imposed limitation, rather than an objective truth, did she begin sharing her work with others, eventually publishing her first novel to critical acclaim.

These constraining beliefs often disguise themselves as practical wisdom or protective measures. They speak in absolutes: "I'm too old to start a new career," "Success requires natural talent," "People like me don't achieve such goals." Yet beneath these seemingly rational statements lie assumptions that deserve careful examination.

Research in cognitive psychology reveals how limiting beliefs create self-fulfilling prophecies. When we believe something lies beyond our reach, we unconsciously behave in ways that reinforce this perception. The brain, seeking to maintain consistency between beliefs and reality, selectively notices evidence that confirms our existing limitations while dismissing contradictory information.

Consider the metaphor of a wild elephant tethered by a thin rope. Despite its tremendous strength, the elephant remains bound because it learned in infancy that it couldn't break free. Similarly, many of our perceived limitations stem from outdated experiences that no longer reflect our current capabilities.

The recognition of limiting beliefs requires developing keen self-awareness. Notice the language you use when facing challenges or opportunities. Phrases like "I could never," "That's impossible for someone like me," or "I always fail at" often signal the presence of limiting beliefs. These verbal patterns serve as breadcrumbs leading to deeper underlying assumptions.

Physical sensations frequently accompany limiting beliefs. A tightening in the chest, shallow breathing, or a sensation of heaviness might emerge when confronting certain possibilities. These bodily responses, developed through past experiences, signal areas where limiting beliefs may be operating beneath conscious awareness.

Cultural and familial inheritances often seed limiting beliefs. Messages absorbed in childhood about money, success, relationships, or personal worth can crystallize into seemingly immutable truths. Yet these inherited beliefs deserve questioning: Do they serve your current reality? Do they align with your authentic aspirations?

The process of recognition requires compassionate curiosity. Rather than immediately attempting to dismantle limiting beliefs, first observe them with gentle attention. What purpose have they served? What fears or uncertainties do they protect? Understanding their origins and perceived benefits creates space for thoughtful examination rather than reactive rejection.

Documentation plays a crucial role in recognition. Keep a belief journal, noting situations that trigger strong reactions of impossibility or inadequacy. Look for patterns in these entries - recurring themes or specific contexts where limiting beliefs appear most active. This written record provides valuable data for identifying and eventually transforming constraining thought patterns.

External feedback often illuminates limiting beliefs we've internalized. Trusted friends or mentors might notice capabilities or possibilities we automatically dismiss. Their perspective can highlight the gap between our perceived limitations and actual potential.

Professional achievements frequently reveal limiting beliefs in stark relief. A promotion might surface beliefs about leadership capability. A creative success might highlight long-held doubts about artistic merit. These moments of achievement create natural opportunities to recognize and question our assumed limitations.

The recognition of limiting beliefs marks the first step toward liberation. Like a prisoner first noticing the bars of their cell, awareness creates the possibility of freedom. This recognition, while sometimes uncomfortable, opens doors to new possibilities and expanded horizons.

Through careful observation and documentation, patterns of limitation become increasingly apparent. These patterns, once recognized, lose their power to operate unconsciously. The very act of recognition begins to loosen their hold, creating space for new beliefs and expanded possibilities to emerge.

Remember that recognition need not immediately lead to transformation. The goal initially is simply to become aware - to notice these subtle yet powerful thought patterns that shape our perceived boundaries. This awareness itself begins to shift our relationship with limiting beliefs, creating the foundation for future growth and expansion.

Understanding Emotional Patterns

Emotions flow through our lives like weather patterns across a landscape, creating distinct rhythms and cycles that shape our daily experience. These emotional patterns, far from being random occurrences, follow discernible sequences that reflect our internal processing of external events, our learned responses, and our deeper psychological structures.

Consider the story of Marcus, a successful architect who noticed his enthusiasm for new projects inevitably transformed into anxiety as deadlines approached, followed by a period of emotional withdrawal after completion. This recurring cycle affected not only his work satisfaction but also his relationships and creative output. Through careful observation, he began to recognize this pattern as a reflection of early experiences with perfectionist parents, allowing him to finally address its root cause.

Our emotional patterns often operate like well-worn paths in a forest. Each time we respond to a situation in a particular way, we deepen these neural tracks, making them easier to follow in future similar circumstances. Research in neuroscience reveals that these emotional highways become increasingly automatic through repetition, influencing our reactions before conscious thought intervenes.

The complexity of emotional patterns mirrors the intricacy of symphonic music. Just as a symphony contains multiple instrumental lines playing simultaneously, our emotional experiences often layer various feelings and responses. Joy might interweave with anxiety, excitement with apprehension, creating rich emotional textures that deserve careful attention and understanding.

Physical sensations serve as reliable indicators of emotional patterns. A tightening chest might herald the onset of anxiety, while a warming sensation around the heart often accompanies moments of genuine connection. Learning to read these bodily signals provides early warning of emotional shifts, allowing for more conscious engagement with recurring patterns.

Environmental triggers play a crucial role in emotional patterning. Certain locations, times of day, or types of interactions might consistently evoke particular emotional responses. These situational cues often operate subconsciously, creating predictable emotional reactions that seem to arise spontaneously but actually follow well-established neural pathways.

The temporal dimension of emotional patterns reveals itself through careful tracking. Some individuals experience predictable mood fluctuations throughout the day, while others notice weekly or monthly cycles. These rhythms often correlate with biological patterns, social schedules, and environmental factors, creating a complex interplay of influences on our emotional state.

Relationship dynamics frequently illuminate our most ingrained emotional patterns. Notice how certain interactions consistently trigger specific emotional responses. These patterns often reflect early attachment experiences and learned coping mechanisms, providing valuable insight into our deeper psychological structure.

Professional contexts offer another rich arena for observing emotional patterns. Presentations might trigger anticipatory anxiety followed by post-performance relief. Conflict situations could spark defensive reactions followed by regret. Recognition of these patterns enables more conscious engagement with workplace challenges.

Cultural and familial inheritance significantly influences our emotional patterns. The ways our families of origin handled emotions - whether through expression, suppression, or transformation - create templates for our own emotional processing. Understanding these inherited patterns allows for more intentional choices about which to maintain and which to modify.

Documentation proves invaluable in pattern recognition. Maintaining an emotion journal, noting not just feelings but their sequences and triggers, reveals recurring themes and cycles. This written record helps identify subtle patterns that might otherwise escape notice, providing data for meaningful change.

The language we use to describe our emotional experiences often reflects and reinforces underlying patterns. Notice recurring metaphors or descriptions in your emotional vocabulary. These linguistic patterns often provide clues to deeper emotional structures and beliefs.

Sleep and physical well-being significantly impact emotional patterns. Fatigue might amplify negative emotional responses, while physical vitality often enhances emotional resilience. Understanding these correlations helps predict and manage emotional fluctuations more effectively.

Seasonal changes frequently influence emotional patterns, creating larger cycles that span months or years. Winter might bring introspection and melancholy, while spring sparks renewal and optimism. Recognition of these broader patterns allows for better preparation and support during challenging periods.

Through careful observation and documentation, emotional patterns become increasingly apparent and manageable. This understanding transforms them from mysterious forces that control us into recognizable rhythms that we can consciously engage with, creating opportunities for growth and transformation.

Releasing Past Narratives

The stories we tell about our past shape our present reality with remarkable precision, much like a sculptor's hands molding clay. These narratives, whether of triumph or tragedy, success or failure, become the lens through which we interpret new experiences and possibilities. Yet many of these stories, crafted in moments of intense emotion or inherited from others' perspectives, may no longer serve our growth or reflect our truth.

Consider Rachel, whose childhood experience of public humiliation during a piano recital crystallized into a narrative about her fundamental inability to perform under pressure. This story, though decades old, continued to influence her professional choices until she recognized its pervasive impact on her current decisions. Through conscious examination, she discovered this narrative represented not an immutable truth but a single moment frozen in time.

Past narratives embed themselves deeply into our psyche through repeated reinforcement. Like grooves worn into a vinyl record, these stories play automatically when triggered by similar circumstances. Research in neuroplasticity reveals that these neural pathways, though well-established, remain malleable throughout our lives, offering hope for meaningful change.

The process of releasing begins with gentle acknowledgment. These stories served a purpose - perhaps protecting us from perceived harm, explaining painful experiences, or maintaining connection with important others. Approaching them with curiosity rather than judgment creates space for new understanding to emerge.

Emotional archaeology proves essential in this process. Carefully excavating the layers of meaning we've attached to past events reveals the difference between what actually occurred and the interpretations we've carried forward. This distinction creates crucial space between event and meaning, allowing for new perspectives to emerge.

Physical sensations often anchor past narratives in our bodies. A tightened throat, shallow breathing, or clenched muscles might signal the activation of old stories. These bodily responses, when noticed with compassion, provide valuable entry points for releasing work. Through conscious breathing and gentle attention, these physical holds begin to loosen.

The language we use to describe our past reveals much about its current influence. Notice phrases like "I always," "I never," or "That's just how I am." These linguistic patterns often signal the presence of limiting narratives that deserve examination. Through careful attention to our words, we begin to identify stories ready for release.

Writing serves as a powerful tool for narrative transformation. Through journaling, we can explore alternative interpretations of past events, examining them from different perspectives and emotional distances. This written exploration often reveals the malleability of memory and the possibility of new meaning-making.

Environmental cues frequently trigger old narratives. Certain locations, relationships, or situations might automatically activate familiar stories. Recognizing these triggers allows us to pause and choose our response rather than automatically replaying established patterns.

The release of past narratives requires not forceful rejection but gentle dissolution. Like ice melting in spring sunshine, these stories naturally transform when held in awareness with patience and compassion. This process allows for integration of their wisdom while releasing their limiting aspects.

Relationships play a crucial role in narrative release. Trusted friends or mentors might offer perspectives that challenge our established stories, creating opportunities for new understanding. Their witness to our current capabilities often highlights the disparity between old narratives and present reality.

Professional achievement frequently catalyzes narrative release. Success in areas previously deemed impossible creates natural opportunities to question other limiting stories. These moments of contradiction between old narrative and current reality open doors for broader transformation.

The process of release creates space for new narratives to emerge - stories that better reflect our current wisdom and capabilities. Like a garden after weeding, this cleared space allows for intentional cultivation of more empowering perspectives and possibilities.

Time itself offers a powerful ally in narrative release. The simple act of viewing past events from our current vantage point often naturally dissolves their emotional charge. Distance provides perspective that allows for gentler interpretation and easier release.

Through conscious attention and compassionate examination, past narratives gradually lose their power to constrain our present choices. This release, though sometimes challenging, creates essential space for new stories to emerge - stories that better serve our current growth and future possibilities.

Reframing Your Story

The art of reframing transforms the very fabric of our lived experience, much like a skilled photographer who discovers fresh beauty by shifting their lens even slightly. Within each life story lies multiple truths, waiting to be illuminated through new perspectives and deeper understanding. Every narrative contains seeds of possibility, dormant until we choose to view our experiences through a different prism.

Take Thomas, a former athlete whose career-ending injury initially represented the death of his dreams. For years, he carried this story as one of devastating loss, until a profound shift in perspective revealed how this very challenge had opened unexpected doors.

His injury led him to discover his gift for coaching, ultimately touching far more lives than he might have as a competitor. Through reframing, his story of loss transformed into one of expanded purpose.

The power of reframing extends beyond simple positive thinking. It involves discovering genuine alternative interpretations that honor both the complexity of our experiences and the multifaceted nature of truth. Research in cognitive psychology demonstrates that our interpretation of events, rather than the events themselves, primarily determines their impact on our lives.

Narrative psychology reveals how the stories we tell shape not only our past but actively create our future. By consciously choosing the lens through which we view our experiences, we literally reshape our neural pathways and create new possibilities for action and understanding. This biological reality underscores the profound impact of reframing on our lived experience.

Consider the metaphor of a gemstone. Each facet reveals different colors and patterns depending on how light strikes its surface. Similarly, our experiences contain multiple facets of meaning, each offering valuable insights and possibilities when viewed from different angles. The art lies in learning to rotate the gem skillfully, discovering new beauty in familiar stories.

Professional setbacks particularly benefit from careful reframing. What appears as rejection might actually represent protection from a poor fit. A missed opportunity often creates space for more aligned possibilities to emerge. Through reframing, apparent failures transform into crucial stepping stones toward more meaningful success.

Language plays a pivotal role in this transformative process. The words we choose to describe our experiences shape how we understand and remember them. Shifting from "I was abandoned" to "I became independent" dramatically alters both the emotional resonance and future implications of past experiences.

Physical spaces often mirror our internal narratives. Notice how your environment might reflect current story patterns. Reframing sometimes requires literal rearrangement of our surroundings, creating external harmony with our evolving internal narrative. This physical reorganization supports and reinforces our shifted perspective.

Relationship dynamics illuminate powerful opportunities for reframing. Conflicts viewed through the lens of mutual growth rather than opposition reveal new possibilities for connection. Challenging relationships reframed as teachers of patience or boundaries transform from sources of frustration into catalysts for development.

The timing of reframing requires delicate consideration. Some experiences need time to be fully felt and integrated before reframing becomes genuinely helpful. Rushing this process can lead to superficial positivity rather than authentic transformation. Honor the natural rhythm of your emotional processing.

Cultural narratives often unconsciously influence our personal stories. Recognizing these broader influences allows us to consciously choose which cultural frames serve our growth and which require questioning or release. This awareness creates space for more authentic personal narrative choices.

Documentation supports sustainable reframing. Journal about experiences from multiple perspectives, actively seeking alternative interpretations that feel both true and empowering. This written exploration creates a record of your evolving understanding and provides anchor points for maintaining shifted perspectives during challenging times.

The process of reframing, while powerful, requires dedication and practice. Like learning a new language, it initially demands conscious effort before becoming natural. Each reframed story strengthens our capacity for flexible thinking and expanded perspective-taking.

Through patient practice and gentle persistence, reframing becomes an invaluable tool for personal transformation. This skill allows us to discover hidden gifts in apparent setbacks, uncover opportunities in challenges, and ultimately craft a life story that empowers rather than constrains our future possibilities.

Building Mental Clarity Practices

Mental clarity emerges through deliberate practice, much like a skilled artisan who daily hones their craft to achieve mastery. The mind, when properly cultivated, becomes a precision instrument capable of razor-sharp focus and profound insight. Yet this clarity requires more than mere wishful thinking – it demands systematic approach and unwavering dedication.

Consider Alexandra, a senior executive whose mind once raced with countless competing priorities. Through developing a robust mental clarity practice, she transformed her cognitive chaos into crystalline focus. Her morning ritual began with twenty minutes of mindful breathing, followed by purposeful journaling that distilled complex challenges into manageable elements. This consistent practice gradually rewired her neural pathways, creating space between stimulus and response.

Research in neuroscience reveals that regular mental clarity practices physically alter brain structure, enhancing neural connections associated with attention and emotional regulation. These changes manifest in measurable improvements in decision-making capacity, creative problem-solving, and overall cognitive performance.

The foundation of mental clarity begins with environmental preparation. Like a photographer carefully cleaning their lens before capturing an important image, we must create conditions conducive to clear thinking. This might mean designating a specific space for contemplative practice, eliminating unnecessary digital distractions, or establishing temporal boundaries that protect our peak cognitive hours.

Breathing serves as an anchor for mental clarity. Conscious breathing patterns – particularly the extended exhale – activate the parasympathetic nervous system, creating a physiological state optimal for clear thinking. This simple yet profound practice becomes especially valuable during moments of mental turbulence or decision-making pressure.

Written reflection amplifies mental clarity through externalization. The act of transferring thoughts from mind to paper creates valuable cognitive distance, allowing for more objective analysis and insight. This practice reveals patterns, contradictions, and possibilities that might otherwise remain hidden in the swirl of mental activity.

Physical movement plays a crucial role in developing mental clarity. Research indicates that regular exercise, particularly activities requiring coordinated movement, enhances cognitive function and reduces mental fog. The body's motion literally helps clear the mind, creating space for sharper thinking and deeper insight.

Dietary choices significantly impact cognitive clarity. Proper hydration, balanced nutrition, and strategic timing of meals create the biological foundation for optimal mental function. Understanding and honoring these physiological requirements supports sustained mental clarity throughout the day.

Sleep hygiene forms another essential pillar of mental clarity practice. Quality rest allows the brain to consolidate information, clear cellular debris, and reset neural circuits. Establishing consistent sleep patterns creates a reliable foundation for daily mental clarity.

Time management strategies support mental clarity through reduced cognitive load. Blocking similar tasks together, establishing clear priorities, and creating intentional breaks prevents the mental fragmentation that often clouds clear thinking. This structured approach conserves cognitive resources for truly important decisions.

Digital awareness becomes increasingly crucial for maintaining mental clarity in our connected world. Strategic use of technology, combined with regular digital detox periods, helps prevent the cognitive scattered that often accompanies constant connectivity. This balanced approach allows us to harness technology's benefits while minimizing its clarity-reducing effects.

Nature exposure provides powerful support for mental clarity practices. Research demonstrates that time spent in natural settings improves attention, reduces mental fatigue, and enhances creative thinking. Even brief encounters with nature can reset our mental state and restore clarity.

Regular review and refinement of clarity practices ensures their continued effectiveness. What works during one life phase might need adjustment in another. This flexible approach, combined with consistent core practices, creates sustainable long-term results.

The development of mental clarity requires patience and persistence. Like watching a pond settle after disturbance, the mind gradually becomes still through regular practice. This stillness reveals depths of insight and understanding previously obscured by surface agitation.

Through dedicated practice and systematic approach, mental clarity becomes not just a temporary state but a stable foundation for navigating life's complexities. This cultivated clarity enables better decisions, deeper relationships, and more meaningful contributions to our chosen endeavors.

Creating Space for Growth

Growth requires space, much like a seed needs room in the soil to extend its roots and unfurl its first tender shoots toward the sun. In our rushed modern lives, we often fill every moment with activity, leaving no room for the essential process of personal expansion. Yet without deliberate space, our potential for transformation remains dormant, waiting for the right conditions to flourish.

Consider the story of James, a brilliant software engineer whose life overflowed with commitments. Despite his desire for creative innovation, his calendar left no room for deep thinking or experimentation. Only after experiencing complete burnout did he recognize the vital importance of creating space in his life. Through intentional pruning of non-essential activities, he discovered that less often yields more.

Creating space operates on multiple dimensions - physical, temporal, mental, and emotional. Each dimension requires careful attention and deliberate cultivation. Like a master gardener preparing soil for precious seeds, we must tend to these spaces with wisdom and patience.

Physical space profoundly influences our capacity for growth. Research in environmental psychology reveals that our surroundings directly impact our thought patterns and emotional states. Cluttered spaces create cluttered minds, while organized environments foster clarity and possibility. This extends beyond mere tidiness to the intentional creation of spaces that inspire and nurture growth.

Temporal space proves equally crucial. Growth requires unhurried time for reflection, experimentation, and integration of new learning. Yet many resist creating this space, fearing the void or feeling guilty about unstructured time. Understanding that fallow periods serve as essential preparation for future abundance helps overcome this resistance.

Mental space emerges through conscious reduction of information overload. Our minds, constantly bombarded with data, require regular clearing to maintain receptivity to new insights and possibilities. This might involve digital detoxes, meditation practices, or simply allowing periods of conscious boredom - a state increasingly rare in our hyper-connected world.

Emotional space provides room for authentic feelings to surface and be processed. Many suppress emotions in the name of productivity or professionalism, creating internal congestion that inhibits growth. Building regular time for emotional expression and processing - through journaling, movement, or creative activities - opens essential pathways for development.

Professional growth particularly benefits from intentional space creation. Innovation and leadership require room for strategic thinking and creative exploration. Yet many organizations and individuals fill every moment with tactical activities, leaving no room for the deeper work that drives meaningful advancement.

Relationship space allows connections to breathe and evolve naturally. Constant contact, whether physical or digital, can paradoxically reduce intimacy by eliminating the space needed for missing, longing, and appreciating others. Strategic distance often strengthens rather than weakens important bonds.

Financial space provides crucial padding for taking calculated risks and pursuing growth opportunities. Building this space requires disciplined saving and thoughtful reduction of unnecessary expenses. This financial buffer creates freedom to explore new directions without paralyzing fear of consequences.

Creating space often requires saying no to good opportunities to make room for great ones. This selective pruning, while sometimes painful, allows remaining elements to flourish more fully. Like a gardener removing excess blooms to strengthen the whole plant, we must sometimes eliminate positive but non-essential activities.

The process of space creation typically feels uncomfortable initially. Our busy culture often equates empty space with wasted time or lost opportunities. Yet this discomfort usually signals approaching breakthrough - the moment when sufficient space allows new growth to emerge.

Environmental design plays a crucial role in maintaining created space. Setting up physical and digital environments that support rather than undermine spaciousness helps sustain long-term growth. This might involve establishing boundaries, creating rituals, or redesigning workspaces to facilitate deeper focus.

Through patient cultivation of space across all life dimensions, we create conditions conducive to sustainable growth. This deliberate spaciousness allows natural expansion while preventing the burnout that often accompanies forced development. Like a well-tended garden, our potential flourishes when given proper room to grow.

Designing Your Environment for Success

The environment we inhabit shapes our behavior, thoughts, and potential with remarkable precision. Like a master architect designing a cathedral, we must thoughtfully craft our surroundings to elevate our capabilities and inspire our highest achievements. Every detail of our environment – from the arrangement of our workspace to the quality of our tools – creates ripples of influence that shape our daily performance and long-term success.

Consider the transformation of Michael, a struggling entrepreneur whose cluttered home office mirrored his scattered thinking. Through strategic environmental redesign – establishing dedicated zones for different activities, optimizing natural light, and eliminating visual noise – he discovered that his surroundings could either amplify or diminish his effectiveness. Within months, his productivity doubled, and creative solutions emerged with surprising ease.

Research in environmental psychology reveals that our physical space profoundly impacts cognitive function, emotional well-being, and behavioral patterns. The brain constantly processes environmental cues, adjusting our internal state in response to external signals. This neurological dance between person and place offers tremendous opportunity for optimizing our performance landscape.

Light plays a crucial role in environmental design for success. Natural illumination regulates our circadian rhythms, enhances mood, and improves cognitive performance. Strategic placement of workspaces near windows, supplemented by carefully chosen artificial lighting, creates an atmosphere conducive to sustained focus and creativity.

Sound shapes our mental state with subtle yet powerful influence. Background noise at specific frequencies can enhance focus, while unexpected disruptions fragment attention and diminish performance. Creating acoustic zones – spaces for concentration, collaboration, and restoration – allows for optimal functioning across different tasks and energy states.

Color psychology offers another tool for environmental optimization. Cool tones promote analytical thinking, while warmer hues stimulate creativity and social connection. Strategic use of color in different areas can support various modes of work and rest, creating a dynamic environment that responds to changing needs.

Physical organization directly impacts mental clarity and decision-making capacity. Every object in our environment either supports or hinders our objectives. Implementing systems for managing physical items – from important documents to daily tools – reduces cognitive load and creates space for higher-level thinking.

Technology integration requires particular attention in environmental design. While digital tools can enhance productivity, their presence often introduces distraction and stress. Creating designated tech-free zones and establishing clear boundaries around device use helps maintain focus while accessing technological benefits.

Ergonomic considerations fundamentally influence our capacity for sustained performance. Proper positioning of furniture and tools prevents physical strain that can diminish mental function. Investment in quality seating, appropriate desk height, and optimal screen placement pays dividends through enhanced endurance and reduced fatigue.

Nature elements introduce vital energy into any environment. Research demonstrates that even simple natural elements – plants, natural materials, or views of outdoor spaces – reduce stress and enhance cognitive function. Incorporating these elements strategically creates micro-moments of restoration throughout the day.

Temperature and air quality significantly impact cognitive performance and energy levels. Proper ventilation, comfortable temperature ranges, and regular air circulation create biological conditions optimal for sustained focus and creativity. These often-overlooked factors can dramatically influence daily performance.

Social dynamics require careful consideration in environmental design. Creating spaces that facilitate both collaboration and privacy allows for optimal functioning across different work modes. The ability to control social interaction – through physical barriers, distance, or designated zones – supports both productivity and relationships.

Personal touches matter more than many realize. Meaningful objects, inspiring artwork, or symbols of past achievements create an emotional connection to space that enhances motivation and persistence. These elements should be chosen thoughtfully to reinforce desired states and behaviors.

Flexibility in environmental design allows adaptation to changing needs and energy levels. Mobile furniture, adjustable lighting, and modular spaces create the ability to shift environments as tasks and requirements evolve. This adaptability supports sustained performance across varying conditions.

Through conscious environmental design, we create external conditions that naturally elevate our internal state and capabilities. Like a well-designed tool that enhances its user's abilities, our environment can become a powerful ally in achieving and sustaining success.

Chapter 3: The Architecture of Personal Growth

Understanding Growth Mindset

The belief that our abilities can be developed through dedication, effort, and learning fundamentally transforms the landscape of personal achievement. This dynamic understanding of human potential, backed by decades of research in psychology and neuroscience, opens doors that fixed thinking patterns keep firmly shut. Like rich soil that nurtures growing seeds, a growth mindset provides the essential foundation for continuous development and expanding possibilities.

Consider the remarkable transformation of Dr. Sarah Chen, a brilliant researcher whose early career was plagued by fear of failure. Her initial belief that scientific ability was innate had created invisible barriers to innovation. Upon discovering research about neuroplasticity and the brain's lifelong capacity for growth, she began viewing challenges as opportunities for development rather than threats to her identity. This shift in perspective led to groundbreaking discoveries in her field, not because she suddenly gained new abilities, but because she finally gave herself permission to stretch beyond perceived limitations.

Neuroscience reveals that learning physically reshapes our brains, creating new neural pathways and strengthening existing connections. Each time we embrace a challenge, persist through difficulty, or learn from feedback, we literally rewire our neural architecture. This biological reality underscores the tremendous power of believing in our capacity for growth and development.

The language of growth mindset creates its own momentum. Phrases like "not yet" rather than "can't" transform seemingly insurmountable obstacles into temporary challenges awaiting solution. This linguistic shift does more than change words – it reshapes our perception of possibility and expands our horizon of achievable goals.

Effort takes on new meaning through the lens of growth mindset. Rather than viewing exertion as proof of inadequacy, we recognize it as the very mechanism of growth – like resistance training that builds mental and emotional muscle. This reframing transforms the experience of difficulty from discouraging to energizing.

Failure, often feared and avoided, becomes a valuable teacher when approached with a growth mindset. Each setback provides specific feedback about areas for improvement and refinement. This perspective allows us to maintain forward momentum even when facing significant challenges, transforming potential stopping points into stepping stones.

Professional environments particularly benefit from growth mindset cultivation. Teams that embrace this perspective demonstrate greater innovation, resilience, and collaborative success. The understanding that abilities can be developed creates psychological safety for taking risks and sharing novel ideas.

Criticism and feedback, often triggers for defensive reactions, become valuable resources for growth when filtered through this developmental lens. Rather than threats to our competence, they represent opportunities to refine our understanding and enhance our capabilities. This shift transforms the emotional experience of receiving feedback from threatening to energizing.

The impact of growth mindset extends beyond individual achievement to influence relationship dynamics. Understanding that interpersonal skills can be developed through conscious effort opens new possibilities for deeper connection and more effective communication. This perspective allows for greater patience with ourselves and others as we navigate social complexity.

Learning strategies naturally evolve under the influence of growth mindset. Instead of avoiding challenges that might expose inadequacy, we actively seek opportunities that stretch our capabilities. This proactive approach to development accelerates progress and expands potential.

Time itself takes on new significance through the lens of growth mindset. Rather than viewing age or experience level as limiting factors, we recognize that development continues throughout life. This perspective frees us from artificial constraints and opens endless possibilities for learning and growth.

Implementing growth mindset requires consistent practice and gentle self-correction when fixed mindset patterns emerge. Like any significant change, this transformation occurs gradually through persistent attention and conscious choice. Each moment offers opportunities to choose growth over limitation, development over stagnation.

Through embracing growth mindset, we unlock our natural capacity for continuous development and expanding achievement. This fundamental shift in perspective transforms challenges from threats into opportunities, effort from burden into pathway, and potential from fixed into limitless.

The Science of Habit Formation

Habits form the invisible architecture of our daily lives, shaping our actions and outcomes with remarkable precision. Recent advances in neuroscience have illuminated the intricate mechanisms through which these behavioral patterns become embedded in our neural circuitry, offering unprecedented insight into their formation and transformation.

Consider the case of Dr. Elena Martinez, a renowned surgeon whose precision in the operating room stemmed not from natural talent alone, but from meticulously cultivated habits. Early in her career, she discovered that excellence emerged not from sporadic brilliant performances, but from the consistent application of carefully designed behavioral sequences. Her story illustrates how deliberate habit formation underlies extraordinary achievement.

Research reveals that habit formation follows a distinct neurological pattern: cue, routine, reward. This trilogy forms the foundation of all habitual behavior, whether beneficial or detrimental. Understanding this sequence allows us to architect new habits with scientific precision, rather than relying on willpower alone.

The brain's basal ganglia plays a crucial role in habit formation, converting sequences of actions into automatic routines. This process, known as chunking, enables complex behaviors to become automatic, freeing cognitive resources for higher-order thinking. Like a skilled composer creating a symphony, we can orchestrate our desired behaviors into seamless sequences.

Timing proves crucial in habit formation. Studies indicate that new behaviors typically require between 21 and 66 days to become automatic, depending on complexity and individual variables. This understanding helps set realistic expectations and maintain commitment through the crucial early stages of habit development.

Environmental design significantly influences habit formation. The physical arrangement of our space can either support or undermine desired behaviors. Strategic placement of cues and removal of obstacles creates a landscape that naturally facilitates positive habit development while discouraging unwanted patterns.

The role of emotion in habit formation cannot be overstated. Strong emotional associations, whether positive or negative, dramatically impact the speed and strength of habit development. Understanding this connection allows us to leverage emotional engagement to reinforce desired behavioral patterns.

Small wins generate momentum in habit formation. Rather than attempting dramatic transformations, research supports the power of minimal viable habits – tiny behaviors that, when consistently executed, create a foundation for larger change. This approach bypasses the resistance often encountered when attempting significant behavioral shifts.

Social context profoundly influences habit development. Studies show that habits spread through social networks, making careful curation of our relationships crucial for successful behavior change. Like a garden requiring specific conditions for growth, habits flourish in supportive social environments.

The concept of habit stacking – attaching new behaviors to existing routines – leverages the brain's natural tendency toward sequential learning. This technique, supported by neurological research, increases the likelihood of successful habit formation by anchoring new behaviors to established patterns.

Tracking mechanisms play a vital role in habit development. Regular measurement and documentation of progress creates accountability and provides valuable data about effectiveness. This scientific approach to habit formation allows for precise adjustments and optimization over time.

The power of identity in habit formation reveals itself through research in behavioral psychology. Habits that align with our self-conception prove more sustainable than those based purely on desired outcomes. This understanding suggests the importance of identity evolution in lasting behavior change.

Recovery protocols deserve particular attention in habit formation. Rather than expecting perfect execution, research supports building resilient habits through planned recovery strategies. This approach transforms potential failure points into opportunities for strengthening behavioral patterns.

Understanding the neuroscience of habit formation empowers us to work with our brain's natural mechanisms rather than against them. Like an engineer working with natural forces rather than opposing them, we can design habits that flow with our neurological tendencies instead of fighting them.

Through deliberate application of these scientific principles, we can craft habits that serve our highest aspirations. This systematic approach transforms habit formation from a mysterious process into a reliable method for personal development and achievement.

Building Resilience

Resilience emerges not as an innate quality, but as a carefully cultivated strength that transforms life's challenges into catalysts for growth. Like a mighty oak that develops its robust character through withstanding countless storms, human resilience grows stronger through each trial we face and overcome.

Consider the remarkable journey of Maya Chen, a startup founder whose first venture collapsed spectacularly, taking with it her savings and initial dreams of entrepreneurial success. Rather than allowing this setback to define her future, Maya approached her failure as a masterclass in business education. She methodically analyzed her mistakes, rebuilt her professional network, and launched a second venture that would eventually transform her industry. Her story exemplifies how resilience manifests not in avoiding failure, but in rising stronger from each setback.

Research in psychological resilience reveals that this quality develops through specific, learnable practices rather than mere endurance of hardship. Studies indicate that resilient individuals share certain cognitive patterns – they view challenges as temporary rather than permanent, specific rather than universal, and manageable rather than overwhelming. This perspective transforms seemingly insurmountable obstacles into navigable challenges.

The neuroplasticity of our brains provides the biological foundation for building resilience. Each time we successfully navigate adversity, we strengthen neural pathways associated with adaptive response patterns. This biological reinforcement creates an upward spiral, where each challenge overcome enhances our capacity to face future difficulties.

Physical resilience underlies emotional fortitude. Regular exercise, adequate sleep, and proper nutrition create the physiological basis for psychological strength. Like a well-maintained vehicle better equipped to handle rough terrain, a healthy body provides the foundation for emotional resilience.

Social connections play a crucial role in resilience development. Studies consistently show that individuals with strong support networks demonstrate greater resilience in facing life's challenges. These relationships provide not just emotional support, but also diverse perspectives and resources for overcoming obstacles.

Professional resilience requires particular attention in today's rapidly changing workplace. The ability to adapt to new technologies, shifting market conditions, and evolving job requirements has become essential for career longevity. This form of resilience demands continuous learning and strategic flexibility.

Emotional regulation stands as a cornerstone of resilience. The capacity to acknowledge and process difficult emotions while maintaining functional behavior distinguishes resilient individuals. This skill allows for experiencing the full range of human emotion without becoming overwhelmed or immobilized.

Purpose and meaning significantly enhance resilience. Research shows that individuals who connect their struggles to larger goals or values demonstrate greater persistence in facing challenges. This sense of purpose transforms mere endurance into meaningful perseverance.

Strategic optimism – distinct from blind positivity – characterizes resilient thinking. This approach combines hopeful outlook with practical problem-solving, creating a balanced perspective that acknowledges difficulties while maintaining focus on potential solutions.

Recovery practices prove essential in building sustainable resilience. Like an athlete who plans rest periods as carefully as training sessions, resilient individuals develop specific strategies for replenishing their emotional and physical resources after periods of intense challenge.

The habit of reflection strengthens resilience by extracting wisdom from experience. Regular contemplation of challenges faced and lessons learned transforms difficulties into valuable learning opportunities, building both knowledge and confidence for future challenges.

Boundary setting plays a vital role in resilience building. Understanding and communicating personal limits prevents the exhaustion that can undermine resilient response patterns. These boundaries create the space necessary for maintaining strength in the face of ongoing challenges.

Through consistent application of these principles, resilience grows from a desired quality into a developed strength. Like a muscle strengthened through regular exercise, our capacity for resilience expands through conscious practice and strategic development.

Mastering Emotional Intelligence

Emotional intelligence emerges as the masterful orchestration of our inner landscape, shaping our interactions, decisions, and ultimate success with profound impact. Like a skilled conductor leading a complex symphony, those who master emotional intelligence harmonize their own emotions while remaining exquisitely attuned to the emotional currents of others.

Consider the transformation of Marcus Chen, a brilliant technologist whose early career was marked by interpersonal tensions despite his exceptional technical abilities. Through dedicated study and practice of emotional intelligence, he discovered that success hinged not merely on cognitive prowess but on the subtle art of emotional awareness and regulation. His journey from technical expert to respected leader illustrates the transformative power of emotional mastery.

Research in neuroscience reveals that emotional intelligence operates through distinct neural networks that can be strengthened through conscious practice. The brain's neuroplasticity enables us to develop these emotional capacities throughout life, much like a musician who refines their ability to distinguish subtle variations in tone and rhythm.

Self-awareness forms the cornerstone of emotional intelligence. This capacity extends beyond simple recognition of emotions to understanding their origins, patterns, and implications. Through careful self-observation, we develop the ability to recognize emotional signals before they escalate into overwhelming responses.

The art of emotional regulation builds upon this foundation of awareness. Like a skilled sailor adjusting their sails to changing winds, emotionally intelligent individuals learn to modulate their responses to match the demands of each situation. This ability enables maintenance of emotional equilibrium even amid challenging circumstances.

Empathy emerges as another crucial dimension of emotional intelligence. This capacity for understanding and sharing the feelings of others creates bridges of connection and understanding. Research indicates that empathetic individuals not only build stronger relationships but also demonstrate superior leadership capabilities across various contexts.

Professional environments particularly benefit from enhanced emotional intelligence. Studies show that emotionally intelligent leaders create more innovative, collaborative, and productive work environments. Their ability to read and respond to emotional undercurrents enables more effective team dynamics and conflict resolution.

The language of emotions requires particular attention in developing emotional intelligence. Like learning a new dialect, we must develop vocabulary and grammar for expressing emotional experiences with precision and nuance. This emotional literacy enables clearer communication and deeper understanding.

Social awareness extends emotional intelligence beyond individual experience to reading and responding to group dynamics. This skill enables navigation of complex social situations with grace and effectiveness, whether in professional settings or personal relationships.

Decision-making transforms through the lens of emotional intelligence. Rather than viewing emotions as obstacles to rational thought, emotionally intelligent individuals integrate emotional data with logical analysis to make more comprehensive and effective choices.

Relationship management flourishes through developed emotional intelligence. The ability to navigate complex interpersonal dynamics, resolve conflicts, and build lasting connections stems directly from this emotional mastery. These skills prove particularly valuable in professional leadership roles.

Stress management becomes more sophisticated through emotional intelligence development. Understanding and responding to emotional pressure points enables more effective coping strategies and greater resilience in challenging situations.

Cultural sensitivity naturally emerges from developed emotional intelligence. The ability to recognize and respect emotional expressions across different cultural contexts becomes increasingly crucial in our interconnected world.

Through dedicated practice and conscious development, emotional intelligence evolves from an abstract concept into a lived reality. This mastery transforms not only our individual experience but our capacity to positively impact the lives of others through deeper understanding and more effective interaction.

Developing Strategic Thinking

Strategic thinking transcends mere planning to encompass a sophisticated approach to understanding and shaping reality. Like a grandmaster in chess who sees not just the next move but entire sequences of possibility, the strategic thinker perceives deeper patterns and broader implications in every situation.

Consider Dr. Isabel Rodriguez, whose groundbreaking cancer research emerged not from random discovery but from methodical strategic analysis. Where others saw disparate data points, she recognized interconnected patterns that suggested novel treatment approaches. Her ability to think strategically transformed seemingly unrelated observations into a coherent framework that revolutionized her field.

The foundations of strategic thinking rest on systematic pattern recognition. Research in cognitive science reveals that expert strategic thinkers process information differently, automatically identifying relationships and implications that others overlook. This capacity, while partially innate, can be deliberately developed through conscious practice and structured analysis.

Temporal perspective plays a crucial role in strategic thinking. Unlike tactical thinking, which focuses on immediate challenges, strategic thought extends across broader time horizons. This expanded temporal view enables recognition of longer-term implications and opportunities that might otherwise remain invisible.

Systems thinking undergirds strategic analysis. Understanding how different elements interact within larger systems enables more effective intervention and innovation. Like an ecologist who comprehends how changing one element affects the entire ecosystem, strategic thinkers grasp the interconnected nature of complex situations.

Scenario planning enhances strategic capability. By systematically exploring multiple possible futures, we develop mental flexibility and prepare for various contingencies. This practice strengthens our ability to recognize early indicators of emerging trends and respond proactively rather than reactively.

Professional contexts particularly benefit from developed strategic thinking. Leaders who think strategically create more sustainable success by anticipating challenges, identifying opportunities, and aligning resources effectively. Their decisions reflect deeper understanding of market dynamics and organizational capabilities.

The art of questioning proves essential in strategic thinking development. Rather than accepting surface appearances, strategic thinkers probe deeper through carefully crafted questions. This investigative approach reveals underlying patterns and possibilities that casual observation might miss.

Environmental scanning becomes second nature to strategic thinkers. They consistently monitor various information sources, seeking early signals of significant changes or opportunities. This vigilant awareness enables more timely and effective response to emerging situations.

Decision-making transforms through strategic thinking. Rather than responding to immediate pressures, strategic thinkers evaluate choices against broader objectives and longer-term implications. This perspective often leads to counter-intuitive but more effective decisions.

Resource allocation improves through strategic thinking. Understanding how different investments of time, energy, and capital might create future advantages enables more effective prioritization. This capability proves particularly valuable in competitive environments where resources are constrained.

Innovation flourishes under strategic thinking. By recognizing patterns and possibilities others miss, strategic thinkers often identify novel solutions to persistent challenges. Their broader perspective enables creative combinations of existing elements into new configurations.

Risk assessment becomes more sophisticated through strategic thinking development. The ability to evaluate multiple potential outcomes and their implications enables better risk management and more confident decision-making under uncertainty.

Through dedicated practice and systematic development, strategic thinking evolves from an occasional activity into a consistent mental framework. This transformation enhances our ability to navigate complexity and create sustainable success across all life domains.

Chapter 4: Actionable Clarity Tools

Decision Making Frameworks

Effective decision-making stands as the cornerstone of personal and professional success, yet many approach this crucial skill haphazardly. The most impactful decisions emerge not from intuition alone, but through structured frameworks that illuminate options and consequences with remarkable clarity.

Consider the transformation of Alexandra Chen, a venture capitalist whose early career was marked by brilliant but inconsistent decisions. Through implementing systematic decision frameworks, she transformed her investment process from intuitive gambling to strategic analysis. Her portfolio's subsequent performance demonstrated the power of structured decision-making approaches.

The OODA Loop framework, originally developed for military strategy, provides a dynamic model for rapid decision-making under pressure. Observe, Orient, Decide, Act - this sequence enables quick yet thorough assessment of changing situations. Like a pilot constantly adjusting to new information, successful decision-makers cycle through these steps continuously, adapting their approach as circumstances evolve.

Cost-benefit analysis, while seemingly straightforward, requires sophisticated application for maximum effectiveness. Beyond simple monetary calculations, this framework demands careful consideration of intangible factors - reputation, relationships, time, energy, and opportunity costs. Expert decision-makers weigh these subtle elements with the same precision they apply to quantifiable metrics.

The Eisenhower Matrix transforms priority-setting through its elegant simplification of urgency versus importance. This framework prevents the common trap of allowing urgent matters to consistently override important ones, ensuring that strategic priorities receive proper attention despite daily pressures.

Scenario planning elevates decision-making by systematically exploring potential futures. Through careful consideration of multiple possibilities - best case, worst case, and most likely outcomes - decision-makers develop more robust strategies that account for uncertainty and change.

The Pre-Mortem technique revolutionizes risk assessment by imagining future failure and working backward to identify potential causes. This reverse chronology often reveals blind spots that forward-looking analysis might miss, enabling more comprehensive risk mitigation strategies.

Values-based decision frameworks ensure alignment between choices and core principles. By explicitly incorporating personal or organizational values into the decision process, these frameworks prevent the common disconnect between stated priorities and actual choices.

The Decision Journal approach transforms individual decision-making capability through systematic documentation and review. By recording decisions, their context, and expected outcomes, then reviewing results over time, decision-makers develop more accurate judgment and refined intuition.

Stakeholder analysis frameworks expand decision consideration beyond immediate impacts to include effects on all involved parties. This broader perspective often reveals opportunities and risks that narrower analysis might overlook, leading to more sustainable decisions.

The Regret Minimization Framework, popularized by successful entrepreneurs, focuses on long-term satisfaction rather than short-term optimization. By considering which choice will create the least regret when viewed from a future perspective, decision-makers often make braver, more aligned choices.

Decision trees provide visual clarity for complex choices with multiple potential outcomes. This framework enables systematic evaluation of various decision paths and their consequences, making probability and risk assessment more intuitive and accurate.

The Implementation Framework bridges the gap between decision and action by addressing execution challenges during the decision process. This integration of strategic and tactical thinking ensures that chosen options are not just theoretically sound but practically achievable.

Through consistent application of these frameworks, decision-making evolves from an anxiety-producing gamble into a confident, systematic process. Like a master chef who knows precisely which technique to apply in each situation, skilled decision-makers select and adapt frameworks to match the specific challenges they face.

Priority Alignment Systems

The mastery of priority alignment transforms chaos into clarity, converting scattered efforts into focused achievement. Like a master conductor who ensures each instrument contributes perfectly to the symphony, effective priority systems orchestrate our various life elements into harmonious progression toward our most significant goals.

Consider the remarkable transformation of Dr. Sarah Chen, a brilliant researcher whose initial career suffered from misaligned priorities. Despite working sixteen-hour days, her most important projects languished while urgent but less significant tasks consumed her attention. Through implementing sophisticated priority alignment systems, she revolutionized not only her productivity but her entire approach to time and energy management.

Research in cognitive psychology reveals that the human brain, despite its remarkable capabilities, struggles to maintain clear priority hierarchies without external support systems. The most effective professionals recognize this limitation and create structured frameworks that externalize priority management, freeing mental resources for higher-level thinking.

The Value-Time Matrix emerges as a cornerstone of priority alignment. This sophisticated approach transcends simple urgency-importance calculations to incorporate long-term value creation and resource optimization. By mapping activities against both immediate impact and future potential, this system illuminates the true priority hierarchy often obscured by daily pressures.

Energy management integrates seamlessly with priority alignment through careful attention to personal peak performance periods. Like an athlete who plans training sessions to maximize physical capacity, effective professionals align their highest-priority tasks with their periods of peak cognitive and creative energy.

The Cascading Goals Framework ensures vertical alignment between daily activities and long-term aspirations. This system creates clear lines of sight from momentary choices to ultimate objectives, enabling confident decision-making even amid competing demands. Each action becomes a deliberate step toward meaningful achievement rather than mere motion.

Regular priority audits maintain system effectiveness through systematic evaluation and adjustment. These reviews reveal subtle misalignments between stated priorities and actual resource allocation, enabling thoughtful recalibration before small discrepancies become significant problems.

Digital tools enhance priority management through automated tracking and reminder systems. However, the most sophisticated practitioners recognize that technology serves rather than drives priority alignment. Their systems integrate digital efficiency while maintaining human wisdom in priority setting and adjustment.

Stakeholder mapping adds crucial dimension to priority alignment by identifying how various activities affect different constituencies. This awareness enables more nuanced priority setting that accounts for both direct outcomes and relationship impacts across professional and personal spheres.

The Flexible Focus system acknowledges the dynamic nature of priorities while maintaining strategic direction. Like a ship adjusting its course while maintaining its destination, this approach allows for tactical flexibility within strategic consistency. It prevents the common error of abandoning important priorities in response to temporary pressures.

Resource allocation transforms through sophisticated priority alignment. Rather than scattered distribution based on immediate demands, resources flow strategically toward highest-value activities. This intentional channeling creates compound benefits through focused investment in truly important areas.

Boundary management emerges naturally from clear priority alignment. When priorities stand in clear hierarchy, saying no to misaligned opportunities becomes not just easier but obviously necessary. This clarity prevents the common trap of overcommitment to low-priority activities.

Through systematic implementation of these principles, priority alignment evolves from aspirational concept to operational reality. Like a well-calibrated compass that consistently points true north, effective priority systems maintain focus on what matters most amid life's constant demands and distractions.

Goal Setting Mastery

Goal setting mastery transcends simple wishful thinking to become an art of purposeful creation. Like an architect who first envisions a magnificent structure in exquisite detail before laying the first stone, masterful goal setters craft their objectives with precision, clarity, and strategic foresight.

Consider Maria Solano, a promising but unfocused entrepreneur whose business floundered despite her remarkable talent. Through developing sophisticated goal-setting practices, she transformed vague aspirations into concrete achievements. Her journey from scattered ambition to focused accomplishment illustrates the transformative power of masterful goal setting.

Research in neuropsychology reveals that well-crafted goals literally reshape our brain's neural pathways. When we define objectives with clarity and emotional resonance, our reticular activating system begins filtering reality differently, highlighting opportunities and resources previously invisible to our awareness.

The architecture of masterful goals combines emotional resonance with tactical precision. Beyond the common SMART criteria, sophisticated goal setting integrates deep purpose with practical execution paths. This marriage of inspiration and implementation creates objectives that both motivate and guide effective action.

Temporal scaffolding plays a crucial role in goal mastery. Like a master builder who understands how each construction phase supports subsequent stages, skilled goal setters create carefully sequenced objectives that build upon each other. This progressive structure transforms ambitious visions into achievable milestones.

Environmental design supports goal achievement through conscious creation of supporting conditions. Physical spaces, social connections, and daily routines align to reinforce rather than undermine goal-directed behavior. This intentional structuring of environment reduces friction and enhances momentum toward desired outcomes.

The paradox of flexibility within commitment marks sophisticated goal setting. While maintaining unwavering commitment to core objectives, masterful goal setters remain flexible about specific implementation paths. This balanced approach enables resilience and adaptation while preserving essential direction.

Measurement systems in masterful goal setting transcend simple metrics to capture meaningful progress indicators. Like a skilled navigator who references multiple data points to confirm position and course, sophisticated goal setters develop nuanced tracking mechanisms that provide accurate feedback about advancement toward objectives.

Integration across life domains characterizes advanced goal setting. Rather than treating professional, personal, and health goals as separate territories, masters create synergistic objectives that support and reinforce each other. This holistic approach maximizes progress while minimizing conflict between different life areas.

Review and refinement protocols maintain goal relevance and effectiveness through systematic evaluation and adjustment. Regular assessment reveals both progress and potential improvements, enabling thoughtful adaptation without losing strategic direction.

The social dimension of goal setting receives careful attention from masters of the craft. They strategically share objectives to create accountability while protecting vulnerable early-stage goals from premature exposure. This balanced approach harnesses social support while maintaining goal integrity.

Implementation planning transforms aspirational goals into actionable strategies. Through detailed consideration of potential obstacles, resource requirements, and necessary capabilities, master goal setters create robust execution frameworks that anticipate and address key challenges.

Celebration criteria define meaningful milestones and appropriate recognition of progress. This intentional acknowledgment of achievement reinforces motivation and maintains momentum while avoiding the common trap of perpetual dissatisfaction with current progress.

Through systematic application of these principles, goal setting evolves from simplex wishful thinking into a sophisticated instrument of personal and professional achievement. Like a master composer who transforms musical inspiration into detailed scores, skillful goal setters convert visions into detailed blueprints for meaningful accomplishment.

Chapter 5: Growth Acceleration Strategies

High Performance Habits

High performance emerges through the deliberate cultivation of specific behavioral patterns that transform ordinary potential into extraordinary achievement. Like a master violinist whose daily practice routines create the foundation for virtuoso performances, individuals who consistently achieve remarkable results operate through carefully developed habits that optimize their capabilities.

Consider Dr. Marcus Chen, whose groundbreaking research in quantum physics stemmed not from sporadic brilliance but from meticulously crafted daily practices. His morning routine began precisely at 4:30 AM with twenty minutes of mindfulness meditation, followed by intense physical exercise and two hours of uninterrupted deep work before most colleagues had begun their day. These habits, maintained with unwavering discipline, created the conditions for breakthrough insights that revolutionized his field.

Research in performance psychology reveals that exceptional achievers share distinct behavioral patterns that transcend individual domains. These habits create a foundation of excellence through systematic optimization of physical energy, mental focus, and emotional resilience. The science demonstrates that consistent application of these patterns literally reshapes neural pathways, enhancing cognitive function and decision-making capabilities.

Strategic recovery emerges as a cornerstone habit of high performers. Unlike the common perception of relentless drive, top achievers recognize that periodic renewal sustains peak performance. They implement deliberate recovery practices with the same precision they bring to active work periods, understanding that restoration directly impacts achievement capacity.

Environmental design plays a crucial role in high-performance habits. Elite performers craft their surroundings to minimize decision fatigue and maximize focused attention. Every element, from workspace organization to digital notifications, undergoes careful evaluation for its impact on performance capacity.

The habit of deliberate preparation distinguishes exceptional achievers. Like Olympic athletes who meticulously plan training cycles, high performers structure their days and weeks to optimize their peak energy periods. This strategic approach to time and energy management ensures maximum impact from every invested hour.

Deep work protocols emerge consistently among high achievers across fields. These individuals develop sophisticated routines that protect their most cognitively demanding work from interruption. Their ability to maintain extended periods of concentrated effort directly correlates with breakthrough achievement.

Relationship curation stands as another critical habit of high performers. They consciously develop and maintain connections that support their growth while diplomatically minimizing exposure to energy-draining interactions. This social optimization creates an environment conducive to sustained excellence.

Data-driven self-reflection characterizes high performers' approach to improvement. They maintain detailed records of their performance patterns, regularly analyzing this information to identify optimization opportunities. This systematic approach to self-awareness enables continuous refinement of their habits and practices.

Physical optimization receives careful attention from high achievers. Understanding the intimate connection between physical vitality and mental performance, they develop sophisticated routines for sleep, nutrition, and exercise. These habits create the physiological foundation for sustained high performance.

Emotional regulation emerges as a crucial habit pattern among exceptional performers. They develop specific practices for maintaining emotional equilibrium under pressure, recognizing that emotional state directly impacts cognitive function and decision quality.

Learning acceleration distinguishes high performers through systematic approaches to skill acquisition. They develop specific routines for rapid mastery of new information and capabilities, constantly expanding their performance capacity through strategic learning practices.

The integration of these habits creates a symphony of excellence that elevates performance beyond ordinary boundaries. Through consistent application and refinement, these patterns become automatic, freeing cognitive resources for higher-level challenges while maintaining exceptional baseline performance.

Strategic Learning Methods

Strategic learning transcends mere information acquisition to become an art of purposeful knowledge synthesis and skill mastery. Like a master chef who understands not just recipes but the underlying principles of cuisine, effective learners develop sophisticated methods that transform raw information into practical wisdom and applicable expertise.

Consider Dr. Elena Santos, whose revolutionary approach to neuroscience emerged not from traditional study methods but from her innovative learning system. She developed a unique synthesis of spaced repetition, concept mapping, and practical application that enabled her to master complex materials at an unprecedented rate. Her breakthroughs in brain plasticity research stemmed directly from her sophisticated approach to learning and integration.

Research in cognitive science reveals that strategic learners process information fundamentally differently from passive recipients. They actively construct knowledge frameworks, deliberately connecting new information to existing understanding while identifying underlying patterns and principles. This architectural approach to learning creates robust, accessible knowledge structures that support both retention and application.

The Feynman Technique emerges as a cornerstone of strategic learning. By explaining complex concepts in simple terms, learners identify and address gaps in their understanding. This method transforms surface familiarity into deep comprehension, enabling both mastery and practical application of new knowledge.

Interleaving practice revolutionizes skill acquisition through strategic variation of learning materials and approaches. Rather than blocking similar topics together, advanced learners deliberately mix different but related concepts, creating stronger neural connections and more flexible understanding.

Elaborative rehearsal elevates learning beyond simple repetition to include meaningful connection and application. Strategic learners constantly ask themselves how new information relates to existing knowledge and potential applications, creating rich networks of understanding that enhance both retention and utilization.

Environmental design plays a crucial role in strategic learning. Advanced practitioners create specific conditions for different types of learning activities, recognizing that environment significantly impacts cognitive processing and retention. This careful curation of learning spaces enhances focus and information processing.

The testing effect becomes a powerful tool in the strategic learner's arsenal. Regular self-assessment not only measures understanding but actively strengthens memory and identifies areas needing additional attention. This systematic approach to evaluation creates a feedback loop that continuously improves learning effectiveness.

Concept mapping transforms information organization through visual representation of knowledge relationships. Strategic learners use this technique to identify connections between ideas, creating comprehensive understanding that transcends simple memorization of isolated facts.

State-dependent learning receives careful attention from sophisticated practitioners. They recognize that physical and emotional states influence both learning and recall, deliberately managing their internal condition to optimize knowledge acquisition and retention.

Pattern recognition training enhances learning efficiency through systematic identification of underlying principles. Strategic learners actively seek commonalities across seemingly different domains, creating mental models that facilitate faster understanding of new information.

Implementation planning distinguishes strategic learning from mere academic exercise. Advanced learners consistently consider how new knowledge will be applied, creating specific plans for practical implementation that enhance both motivation and retention.

Through systematic application of these methods, learning transforms from passive reception into active creation of expertise. Like a master architect who understands both theoretical principles and practical application, strategic learners develop sophisticated approaches that maximize their educational investment while creating lasting, applicable knowledge.

Personal Innovation Practices

Innovation at the personal level manifests through deliberate practices that transform ordinary thinking into extraordinary breakthroughs. Like an artist who develops unique techniques to create masterpieces, individuals who consistently generate novel solutions cultivate specific habits that enhance their creative capacity and problem-solving abilities.

Consider Marina Chen, a renowned architect whose revolutionary sustainable building designs emerged from her distinctive approach to innovation. Each morning, she engaged in what she called "possibility thinking" - a carefully structured practice of challenging fundamental assumptions about construction and environmental impact. This systematic approach to questioning established norms led to breakthrough solutions that redefined eco-friendly architecture.

Research in cognitive science reveals that personal innovation follows predictable patterns that can be deliberately cultivated. Studies demonstrate that innovative thinking emerges not from random inspiration but through specific mental practices that enhance cognitive flexibility and creative problem-solving capabilities.

Cross-pollination stands as a cornerstone of personal innovation practice. By deliberately exposing themselves to diverse fields and perspectives, innovative thinkers create unique mental connections that spark novel solutions. This intentional cultivation of varied influences generates fresh insights through unexpected combinations of ideas.

Constraint mapping transforms limitations into catalysts for creativity. Rather than viewing restrictions as obstacles, skilled innovators use them as creative frameworks that challenge conventional thinking and force novel approaches. This deliberate embrace of constraints often yields more innovative solutions than unlimited freedom.

Rapid prototyping accelerates innovation through quick implementation of ideas in simplified form. Instead of waiting for perfect conditions or complete understanding, effective innovators create minimal viable versions of their concepts, learning and refining through direct experience rather than theoretical planning.

The practice of systematic observation distinguishes truly innovative thinkers. They develop sophisticated methods for noticing details and patterns that others overlook, creating rich mental databases of potential solutions and unexpected connections. This deliberate attention to detail fuels their innovative capacity.

Incubation periods receive careful attention from skilled innovators. They recognize that breakthrough insights often emerge after periods of apparent stagnation, deliberately incorporating rest and reflection into their creative process. This strategic use of downtime enhances innovative thinking.

Question storming revolutionizes problem-solving through systematic inquiry. Instead of rushing to solutions, innovative thinkers develop the practice of generating multiple perspectives through carefully crafted questions. This approach often reveals overlooked opportunities and novel approaches.

Environmental design plays a crucial role in personal innovation. Advanced practitioners create specific spaces and conditions that enhance their creative thinking, recognizing that physical environment significantly impacts innovative capacity. This careful curation of surroundings supports breakthrough thinking.

Documentation transforms fleeting insights into lasting innovations through systematic capture and development of ideas. Skilled innovators maintain detailed records of their thoughts and observations, creating rich resources for future innovation while identifying patterns in their creative process.

Through dedicated application of these practices, personal innovation evolves from occasional insight into consistent capability. Like a master chef who develops signature techniques through years of experimentation, individuals who cultivate these practices transform their innovative potential into reliable creative output.

Energy Management

Energy emerges as the fundamental currency of achievement, yet most individuals focus on managing time while neglecting this more crucial resource. Like a master conductor who understands the ebb and flow of an orchestra's dynamics, those who excel in life learn to orchestrate their energy with precise intention and sophisticated awareness.

Consider Dr. Sarah Chen, a pioneering researcher whose groundbreaking discoveries stemmed not from working longer hours but from mastering her energy cycles. Through careful observation and strategic planning, she identified her peak cognitive periods and aligned her most demanding work with these natural rhythms. This sophisticated approach to energy management transformed her productivity and creative output while actually reducing her working hours.

Research in chronobiology reveals that human energy follows distinct patterns, with predictable peaks and valleys throughout the day. Understanding and working with these natural rhythms, rather than fighting against them, creates the foundation for sustained high performance across all life domains.

Physical energy forms the bedrock of all other energy types. Like a high-performance vehicle requiring premium fuel and regular maintenance, our bodies demand specific conditions for optimal functioning. Strategic nutrition, targeted exercise, and quality sleep create the physiological foundation for sustained energy availability.

Mental energy requires particularly careful stewardship. Cognitive demands deplete our resources in predictable patterns, yet most people ignore these rhythms until forced to stop by complete exhaustion. Advanced practitioners learn to recognize subtle signs of mental fatigue and implement strategic renewal practices before reaching critical depletion.

Emotional energy significantly impacts overall capacity yet often receives minimal attention. Understanding that emotional states profoundly affect performance, sophisticated energy managers develop specific practices for maintaining emotional equilibrium. This emotional stability creates a reservoir of energy for handling life's inevitable challenges.

The architecture of energy management involves strategic oscillation between expenditure and renewal. Like an athlete who understands the vital role of recovery in performance enhancement, effective energy managers build deliberate renewal periods into their daily and weekly rhythms.

Environmental design plays a crucial role in energy optimization. Physical spaces, social interactions, and daily routines either enhance or deplete our energy reserves. Advanced practitioners carefully curate their surroundings to support rather than drain their energy systems.

Relationship energy demands particular attention in our interconnected world. Social interactions can either energize or deplete us, making conscious curation of our relationship portfolio essential for sustained energy availability. This strategic approach to social energy management often requires difficult but necessary choices about time and attention allocation.

Digital energy management becomes increasingly crucial in our technology-saturated environment. Understanding how different types of digital engagement affect our energy systems enables more strategic use of technology while preventing the endemic energy drain of constant connectivity.

Seasonal energy patterns receive careful attention from sophisticated practitioners. Like farmers who understand the rhythm of planting and harvest seasons, effective energy managers recognize and work with natural cycles of high and low energy throughout the year.

Through systematic application of these principles, energy management evolves from reactive crisis response into proactive resource optimization. Like a master chess player who thinks several moves ahead, advanced energy managers anticipate and prepare for varying energy demands while maintaining consistent high performance.

The integration of these various energy systems creates a symphony of sustained capability, enabling remarkable achievement without the burnout that often accompanies high performance. This sophisticated approach to energy management transforms not just individual capability but the entire experience of engaged living.

Time Mastery

The relentless ticking of the clock is a constant companion, a reminder that time waits for no one. Yet, for those who have mastered its ebb and flow, time becomes an ally - a powerful resource to be harnessed and optimized. In this chapter, we will uncover the secrets to reclaiming control over the very essence of our existence, unlocking the keys to Time Mastery.

At the heart of time mastery lies a fundamental shift in perspective. Rather than viewing time as a constraint, we must come to see it as a canvas upon which we paint the masterpiece of our lives. By cultivating a deep understanding of how time operates, we can learn to work with its natural rhythms, bending it to our will without ever breaking its sacred rules.

One of the most crucial skills in time mastery is the art of prioritization. In a world that bombards us with endless demands and distractions, the ability to discern the truly essential from the merely urgent is paramount. Through the practice of ruthless prioritization, we can eliminate the trivial and focus our energies on the tasks and activities that truly move the needle, propelling us closer to our most cherished goals.

Equally important is the mastery of task management. Time is a finite resource, and how we allocate it can make or break our progress. By implementing robust systems and strategies, we can ensure that every minute is spent productively, minimizing the time-sinks that so often derail our best-laid plans. From the judicious use of to-do lists and calendars to the strategic deployment of automation and delegation, the tools of time mastery are within reach of all who seek to wield them.

Yet, time mastery is not merely a practical exercise; it is also a deeply personal journey of self-discovery. As we learn to navigate the currents of time, we uncover profound insights about our own habits, tendencies, and limitations. By confronting our procrastination, our perfectionism, and our penchant for multitasking, we can develop the self-awareness necessary to make the profound shifts required for true time mastery.

At the culmination of this journey lies the ultimate prize: the freedom to live a life of purpose, passion, and fulfillment. When we have mastered the art of time, we are no longer slaves to the clock, but rather its maestros, conducting the symphony of our lives with precision and grace. We can devote ourselves to the pursuits that ignite our spirits, secure in the knowledge that every moment is being leveraged to its fullest potential.

Time mastery is not merely a skill to be learned, but a mindset to be cultivated. It requires a willingness to challenge our preconceptions, to embrace change, and to relentlessly pursue excellence. Yet, for those who embark upon this transformative path, the rewards are immeasurable. Time, once a relentless adversary, becomes a loyal companion, a tool to be wielded in the service of our highest aspirations.

So let us begin the journey, confident in the knowledge that the keys to time mastery lie within our grasp. With unwavering focus and a deep commitment to personal growth, we can unlock the secrets of the clock, forever altering the trajectory of our lives.

Chapter 6: Integration and Implementation

Creating Your Growth Blueprint

Embarking on a transformative journey of personal growth requires more than mere determination - it demands a clear and comprehensive blueprint. Like any grand architectural endeavor, the foundation upon which we build our dreams must be meticulously planned, strategically laid, and rigorously maintained. In this chapter, we will uncover the essential elements of Creating Your Growth Blueprint, equipping you with the tools and insights necessary to architect the future you've always envisioned.

At the heart of any effective growth blueprint lies a steadfast commitment to self-discovery. It is only by peeling back the layers of our subconscious, unearthing our deepest desires and most deeply-rooted fears, that we can begin to chart a course towards meaningful, lasting change. Through the practice of introspection, meditation, and honest self-reflection, we can cultivate the self-awareness required to make informed, empowered choices about the direction of our lives.

Hand-in-hand with self-discovery comes the critical task of goal-setting. Far too often, our attempts at personal growth founder upon the rocky shoals of vague aspirations and haphazard planning. By translating our loftiest ambitions into concrete, measurable objectives, we imbue our journey with a sense of purpose and momentum. Whether it's mastering a new skill, achieving financial independence, or unlocking the secrets of fulfilling relationships, the process of crafting a growth blueprint demands that we crystallize our vision into tangible, time-bound targets.

Of course, the creation of a robust growth blueprint extends far beyond the mere identification of goals. True mastery lies in the meticulous construction of the roadmap that will guide us towards their realization. This entails the careful mapping of milestones, the strategic deployment of resources, and the implementation of accountability measures to ensure that we stay on track. It is only by breaking down our grand ambitions into a series of manageable, actionable steps that we can transform the abstract into the achievable.

As we navigate the terrain of our growth blueprint, we must also be prepared to confront the inevitable obstacles that arise. From the siren call of self-doubt to the seductive allure of procrastination, the forces that seek to undermine our progress are legion. Yet, it is precisely in these moments of challenge that we have the opportunity to cultivate the resilience and adaptability that are the hallmarks of true personal growth. By developing a repertoire of strategies for overcoming roadblocks, whether through the application of positive psychology, the mobilization of our support systems, or the mastery of time-management techniques, we equip ourselves with the fortitude required to weather any storm.

Ultimately, the creation of a growth blueprint is not merely an intellectual exercise, but a profound act of self-empowerment. In committing our dreams to paper, we imbue them with a tangibility and a sense of inevitability that can catalyze profound transformation. As we bring our blueprint to life, step by measured step, we bear witness to the unfolding of our own potential, the blossoming of a vision that was once nothing more than a glimmer in our mind's eye.

So let us embrace the challenge of Creating Your Growth Blueprint, confident in the knowledge that the rewards of our efforts will be manifold. For in the pursuit of personal growth, we do not merely improve ourselves - we inspire those around us, we leave an indelible mark upon the world, and we become the architects of our own destiny.

Building Support Systems

No person is an island, and the journey towards personal growth and fulfillment is no exception. In fact, the strength and resilience required to weather the storms of transformation are often rooted in the fertile soil of a robust support system. In this chapter, we will explore the art of Building Support Systems - a crucial component in unlocking your full potential and cultivating a life of meaning and purpose.

At the foundation of any effective support system lies a deep understanding of our own needs and vulnerabilities. It is only by gaining clarity on the areas in which we require assistance, encouragement, and accountability that we can begin to curate a network of individuals and resources tailored to our unique circumstances. Whether it's the emotional sustenance provided by close friends and family, the technical expertise of mentors and coaches, or the camaraderie of like-minded communities, the building blocks of our support system must be carefully selected to address our most pressing challenges.

Of course, the mere identification of our support needs is merely the first step on the path to creating a transformative network. The true test lies in the art of cultivation - the nurturing of these relationships through open communication, unwavering trust, and a genuine commitment to mutual growth. It is in these moments of vulnerability, when we shed the masks of self-reliance and share our innermost struggles, that the seeds of our support system take root and flourish.

One of the most powerful tools in Building Support Systems is the strategic deployment of accountability partners. These trusted allies, whether they be friends, family members, or professional coaches, serve as beacons of accountability, challenging us to stay the course and holding us responsible for the commitments we make to ourselves. By enlisting the aid of these steadfast companions, we not only heighten our chances of success, but we also cultivate the self-discipline and resilience required to navigate the inevitable setbacks that arise on the journey of personal transformation.

Equally important in the art of Building Support Systems is the cultivation of community. In an age of increased isolation and digital disconnection, the power of belonging to a supportive, like-minded group cannot be overstated. Whether it's a weekly mastermind, a monthly book club, or a quarterly retreat, these spaces of shared experience, collective wisdom, and mutual encouragement can serve as wellsprings of inspiration, motivation, and accountability.

As we weave the tapestry of our support system, it is crucial to remember that the strength of these connections is not measured solely in their quantity, but in their quality. It is far better to maintain a small, tight-knit circle of trusted confidants than to surround ourselves with a vast network of superficial relationships. By investing the time and energy required to nurture deep, meaningful bonds, we ensure that our support system is not merely a collection of acquaintances, but a community of kindred spirits committed to our shared growth and prosperity.

Ultimately, the act of Building Support Systems is not merely a practical exercise, but a profound testament to our willingness to be vulnerable, to seek help, and to embrace the transformative power of human connection. For in the darkest moments of our journey, when the weight of our burdens threatens to pull us under, it is the unwavering support of our trusted allies that provides the buoyancy required to keep us afloat. And in those shining moments of triumph, when we stand tall and proud, it is the collective celebration of our support network that lends wings to our dreams, propelling us ever higher towards the realization of our full potential.

Measuring Progress

Embarking upon a journey of personal transformation can be an exhilarating, yet daunting endeavor. Amidst the whirlwind of change and the allure of ambitious goals, it is all too easy to lose sight of the critical role that Measuring Progress plays in the realization of our dreams. In this chapter, we will explore the art of tracking our growth, celebrating our triumphs, and using data-driven insights to chart an unwavering course towards the future we envision.

At the heart of effective progress measurement lies a fundamental shift in perspective. Rather than viewing the milestones of our journey as distant, unattainable peaks, we must learn to embrace them as stepping stones - tangible markers that signify the steady accumulation of our efforts. By cultivating the habit of regular self-assessment, we imbue our growth with a sense of tangibility, allowing us to objectively gauge our progress and make informed adjustments to our strategies as needed.

One of the most powerful tools in the arsenal of progress measurement is the strategic deployment of key performance indicators (KPIs). These quantifiable metrics, tailored to the unique contours of our personal growth blueprint, serve as beacons of clarity, illuminating the areas in which we are excelling and the domains that require greater attention. Whether it's the number of meditation sessions completed, the percentage increase in savings, or the improvement in interpersonal communication skills, the judicious selection of KPIs empowers us to transform the abstract into the actionable, lending structure and accountability to our transformation.

Of course, the mere identification of KPIs is only the first step in the journey of Measuring Progress. The true power lies in the consistent, disciplined tracking of these metrics, a practice that allows us to discern patterns, identify areas of weakness, and make strategic adjustments to our approach. By meticulously recording our progress, whether through the use of digital tools, analog journals, or a combination thereof, we imbue our growth with a sense of tangibility, transforming the ephemeral into the enduring.

As we navigate the ebb and flow of our transformation, it is essential to remember that progress is not always linear. Inevitably, there will be moments of stagnation, setbacks, and even regression - times when the climb appears insurmountable and the summit hopelessly distant. Yet, it is precisely in these moments that the power of Measuring Progress becomes most pronounced. By maintaining a steadfast commitment to data-driven self-reflection, we cultivate the resilience and adaptability required to weather any storm, emerging stronger, wiser, and more determined than ever before.

Ultimately, the act of Measuring Progress is not merely a practical exercise, but a profound act of self-love and self-empowerment. In charting the incremental steps of our transformation, we bear witness to the unfolding of our own potential, the blossoming of a vision that was once nothing more than a glimmer in our mind's eye. And as we celebrate each hard-won victory, no matter how small, we ignite the spark of hope that will carry us ever onwards, fueling the conviction that the realization of our grandest dreams is not merely possible, but inevitable.

So let us embrace the challenge of Measuring Progress, confident in the knowledge that the rewards of our efforts will be manifold. For in the pursuit of personal growth, we do not merely improve ourselves - we inspire those around us, we leave an indelible mark upon the world, and we become the architects of our own destiny.

Adapting to Change

The only constant in life is change, a truth that has echoed through the ages. Yet, for many, the prospect of adaptation in the face of upheaval can feel like traversing uncharted waters, fraught with the perils of uncertainty and the temptation to cling to the familiar. In this chapter, we will explore the art of Adapting to Change, uncovering the strategies and mindsets required to not merely survive, but thrive amidst the tides of transformation.

At the heart of effective adaptation lies a fundamental shift in perspective - a willingness to embrace the inherent unpredictability of the human experience. Rather than viewing change as an adversary to be conquered, we must learn to perceive it as an ally, a catalyst for growth and reinvention. By cultivating a mindset of flexibility, curiosity, and resilience, we imbue ourselves with the tools necessary to navigate even the most turbulent of storms, emerging stronger, wiser, and more aligned with our deepest values.

One of the most powerful enablers of adaptation is the practice of cultivating a growth mindset. In a world that often rewards rigidity and the veneration of the status quo, it is all too easy to succumb to the siren call of complacency, shunning the very opportunities for transformation that hold the keys to our fulfillment. By embracing a worldview that celebrates learning, experimentation, and the ongoing refinement of our skills and perspectives, we liberate ourselves from the shackles of fear and self-limitation, positioning ourselves to seize the abundant possibilities that change invariably brings.

Of course, the journey of adapting to change is not without its challenges. Faced with the dissolution of familiar routines, the loss of cherished relationships, or the upheaval of our professional trajectories, it is natural to experience a profound sense of disorientation and grief. Yet, it is in these very moments of upheaval that the true mettle of our adaptability is forged. By cultivating a repertoire of coping mechanisms - from the soothing balm of mindfulness to the fortifying power of social connection - we equip ourselves with the resilience required to weather any storm, emerging from the crucible of change with a renewed sense of purpose and clarity.

Equally essential in the art of Adapting to Change is the strategic deployment of goal-setting and action planning. Rather than allowing the tides of transformation to cast us adrift, we must learn to harness their currents, using them to propel us towards the realization of our most cherished aspirations. By defining clear, measurable objectives and breaking them down into a series of manageable steps, we imbue the process of adaptation with a sense of structure and momentum, transforming the abstract into the tangible.

Ultimately, the mastery of Adapting to Change is not merely a practical exercise, but a profound invitation to embrace the fullness of the human experience. For in the crucible of transformation, we are afforded the opportunity to shed the vestiges of our former selves, to confront our deepest fears and insecurities, and to emerge reborn, empowered to live with greater intentionality, authenticity, and purpose. It is in these moments of upheaval that we discover the true depths of our resilience, the wellspring of our courage, and the boundless potential that lies within.

So let us embark upon the journey of Adapting to Change, confident in the knowledge that the rewards of our efforts will be manifold. For in the face of uncertainty, we find the fertile soil in which the seeds of our greatest triumphs take root and flourish, transforming the challenges of today into the milestones of tomorrow.

Chapter 7: Sustaining Long Term Success

The Continuity Framework

Amidst the ever-shifting tides of modern life, the human experience has become increasingly fragmented, with disparate facets of our identities and aspirations often seeming to pull us in opposing directions. Yet, it is in the recognition of this very duality that we uncover the key to unlocking our fullest potential - a concept we shall explore in depth through the lens of The Continuity Framework.

At the heart of this transformative approach lies the understanding that personal growth is not a linear journey, but rather a tapestry woven from the intertwining threads of our multifaceted selves. Rather than viewing our aspirations, our values, and our sense of purpose as isolated domains, The Continuity Framework encourages us to embrace the inherent interconnectedness that lies at the core of the human experience.

By cultivating a holistic perspective that honors the fluidity of our individual narratives, we empower ourselves to transcend the artificial boundaries that so often constrain our growth. No longer must we compartmentalize our professional ambitions, our creative passions, and our spiritual yearnings, relegating each to its own silo. Instead, we are liberated to perceive these elements as integral, mutually reinforcing components of a greater whole - a symphony of self-actualization in which each note, no matter how distinct, contributes to the harmonious unfolding of our truest selves.

The true power of The Continuity Framework, however, lies in its ability to transform the way we approach the inevitability of change. For in a world that so often rewards rigidity and the veneration of the status quo, it is all too easy to succumb to the seductive pull of stagnation, shunning the very opportunities for transformation that hold the keys to our fulfillment. Yet, by embracing a worldview that celebrates the fluidity of our identities, we imbue ourselves with the adaptability required to navigate even the most turbulent of storms, emerging stronger, wiser, and more aligned with our deepest values.

At the foundation of this transformative approach lies the practice of self-reflection - a deep dive into the wellsprings of our consciousness that allows us to uncover the threads of continuity that weave through the tapestry of our lives. Through the cultivation of mindfulness, the exploration of our personal narratives, and the unearthing of our core values, we develop the self-awareness necessary to perceive the underlying unity that connects the disparate facets of our being.

Armed with this profound understanding, we are then empowered to engage in the intentional, strategic forging of our future selves. By aligning our short-term goals and daily habits with our long-term aspirations, we imbue our growth with a sense of coherence and purpose, transforming the abstract into the tangible. Whether it's the pursuit of a new career path, the cultivation of a creative passion, or the deepening of our spiritual practices, The Continuity Framework provides us with the tools to weave these elements into a seamless tapestry of self-actualization.

Ultimately, the mastery of The Continuity Framework is not merely a practical exercise, but a profound invitation to embrace the fullness of the human experience. For in recognizing the inherent unity that underpins our seemingly fragmented lives, we unlock the keys to a life of greater fulfillment, authenticity, and purpose. It is in this state of holistic self-awareness that we discover the wellspring of our resilience, the depths of our creativity, and the boundless potential that lies within.

So let us embark upon this transformative journey, confident in the knowledge that the rewards of our efforts will be manifold. For in the embrace of The Continuity Framework, we do not merely improve ourselves - we inspire those around us, we leave an indelible mark upon the world, and we become the architects of our own destiny.

Evolution of Goals

The road to self-actualization is paved not with a single, unwavering destination, but with the ebb and flow of evolving goals - a tapestry of aspirations that shift, expand, and refine themselves in lockstep with the unfolding of our personal narratives. In this chapter, we will delve into the dynamic nature of goal-setting, uncovering the strategies and mindsets required to harness the power of this ever-changing landscape and transform it into the cornerstone of our growth.

At the heart of the Evolution of Goals lies an understanding that our dreams and ambitions are not static, monolithic constructs, but rather living, breathing entities that respond to the ebbs and flows of our lived experiences. Just as the tides of the ocean ebb and flow in sync with the rhythms of the moon, so too do our innermost yearnings ebb and flow in response to the myriad forces that shape our existence. It is in the recognition of this fundamental truth that we unlock the keys to navigating the currents of personal transformation with grace and intentionality.

One of the most crucial facets of the Evolution of Goals is the ability to cultivate a mindset of adaptability. In a world that so often rewards rigid adherence to a predetermined path, it can be tempting to cling to our goals with an iron grip, shunning the very opportunities for growth and reinvention that lie in wait. Yet, it is only by embracing a worldview that celebrates the fluidity of our aspirations that we position ourselves to seize the abundant possibilities that change invariably brings.

Through the practice of regular self-reflection and the ongoing refinement of our vision, we imbue our growth with a sense of dynamism, allowing us to seamlessly pivot in response to the shifting tides of our circumstances. Whether it's the loss of a cherished relationship, the dissolution of a long-held career path, or the emergence of a newfound passion, the mastery of the Evolution of Goals grants us the agility required to not merely weather the storms of change, but to harness them as the very catalysts of our transformation.

Of course, the journey of goal evolution is not without its challenges. As we navigate the ebb and flow of our aspirations, we may find ourselves confronted with feelings of disorientation, self-doubt, and even a profound sense of loss. Yet, it is precisely in these moments of upheaval that the true power of the Evolution of Goals becomes most apparent. By cultivating a repertoire of coping mechanisms - from the soothing balm of mindfulness to the fortifying power of community - we equip ourselves with the resilience required to weather any storm, emerging from the crucible of change with a renewed sense of purpose and clarity.

Legacy Building

Indelibly etched upon the tapestry of human existence are the legacies we leave behind - the intangible gifts we bequeath to future generations, the enduring ripples of our lives that transcend the finite boundaries of our own mortality. In this chapter, we will explore the art of Legacy Building, uncovering the strategies and mindsets required to craft a lasting imprint upon the world around us.

At the heart of legacy lies the recognition that our actions, our values, and our stories possess a power that extends far beyond the confines of our individual lifespans. With each decision we make, each relationship we nurture, and each idea we give voice to, we weave the threads of our existence into a living, breathing testament to the human experience. It is this awareness that imbues the process of Legacy Building with a profound sense of purpose and urgency, challenging us to cultivate a heightened consciousness of the impact we create, both in the present and for generations yet to come.

One of the most crucial facets of legacy building is the art of self-reflection. By engaging in a deep exploration of our personal narratives, our core values, and our most cherished aspirations, we empower ourselves to discern the lasting imprint we wish to leave upon the world. Whether it's the establishment of a charitable foundation, the preservation of a family heirloom, or the creation of a body of artistic or intellectual work, the clarity of vision we achieve through self-examination is the cornerstone upon which our enduring legacies are built.

Equally essential in the realm of Legacy Building is the strategic deployment of goal-setting and action planning. Rather than allowing the passage of time to dictate the shape and scope of our legacies, we must learn to harness the power of intentionality, imbuing our long-term visions with a sense of structure and momentum. By breaking down our grandest aspirations into a series of measurable milestones, we equip ourselves with the roadmap required to transform the abstract into the tangible, ensuring that the legacy we create is one that is both impactful and enduring.

Of course, the journey of Legacy Building is not without its challenges. As we navigate the ebb and flow of our lives, we may find ourselves confronted with unexpected obstacles, from the loss of loved ones to the upheaval of our professional trajectories. Yet, it is precisely in these moments of adversity that the true measure of our legacy-building prowess is tested. By cultivating a repertoire of resilience-building techniques, from the practice of gratitude to the embrace of community, we equip ourselves with the fortitude required to weather any storm, emerging stronger, wiser, and more resolute in our commitment to the lasting impact we aim to create.

Ultimately, the mastery of Legacy Building is not merely a practical exercise, but a profound invitation to transcend the finite boundaries of our own existence. For in the act of crafting an enduring imprint upon the world, we do not merely improve ourselves - we inspire those around us, we leave an indelible mark upon the tapestry of human civilization, and we become the conduits through which the aspirations and dreams of generations yet unborn find their voice. It is in this state of legacy-consciousness that we unlock the keys to a life of greater purpose, fulfillment, and profound meaning.

So let us embark upon the journey of Legacy Building, confident in the knowledge that the rewards of our efforts will be manifold. For in the embrace of this transformative endeavor, we do not merely leave behind a testament to our own lives - we create the foundation upon which the future of humanity is built.

Mentoring Others

The alchemy of mentorship is woven from the most luminous strands of the human experience - the intertwining of wisdom and wonder, of guidance and growth, of legacies passed and futures forged. In this chapter, we will delve into the transformative power of Mentoring Others, uncovering the strategies, mindsets, and responsibilities that underpin this profound calling.

At the heart of impactful mentorship lies a fundamental shift in perspective - a willingness to view our own hard-won lessons, our accumulated knowledge, and our hard-earned triumphs not as closely guarded possessions, but as the raw materials with which we can sculpt the futures of those who seek our counsel. For in the act of sharing our stories, our insights, and our most cherished values, we do not merely impart information; we kindle the flames of inspiration, empowering others to transcend the limits of their own perceived capabilities.

Yet, the role of the mentor extends far beyond the mere transmission of knowledge. Indeed, it is in the fostering of deep, meaningful connections that the true magic of mentorship resides. By cultivating an environment of trust, empathy, and unwavering support, we create the fertile soil in which the seeds of our protégés' dreams can take root and flourish. Through the thoughtful posing of probing questions, the gentle nudging towards self-discovery, and the steadfast championing of our mentees' aspirations, we become the guiding lights that illuminate the path forward, even in the face of the most daunting obstacles.

Of course, the journey of mentorship is not without its inherent challenges. As we invest our time, our energy, and our very selves in the growth and development of another, we open ourselves to the risk of disappointment, of setbacks, and of the inevitable ebb and flow of human progress. Yet, it is precisely in these moments of trial that the true measure of a mentor's character is revealed. By embracing a mindset of flexibility, resilience, and an unshakable belief in the potential of those we serve, we demonstrate the very qualities that inspire our mentees to push past their perceived limitations and achieve their grandest dreams.

Equally essential in the art of Mentoring Others is the cultivation of a spirit of humility and continuous learning. For even as we impart the wisdom of our own experiences, we must remain ever-cognizant of the fact that the role of mentor is not one of omniscience, but rather of partnership - a symbiotic exchange in which both parties are afforded the opportunity to grow, to evolve, and to transcend the boundaries of their individual perspectives. It is in this state of mutual respect and intellectual curiosity that the most transformative mentorships take root, yielding rich harvests of insight, innovation, and profound personal growth.

Ultimately, the mastery of Mentoring Others is not merely a professional pursuit, but a profound calling that speaks to the very essence of the human experience. For in the act of guiding others towards the realization of their full potential, we do not merely improve the lives of our protégés - we enhance the collective fabric of our society, we leave an indelible mark upon the world, and we become the living embodiments of the legacies we wish to leave behind. It is in this state of legacy-consciousness that we unlock the keys to a life of greater purpose, fulfillment, and profound meaning.

So let us embrace the transformative power of Mentoring Others, confident in the knowledge that the rewards of our efforts will be manifold. For in the cultivation of thriving mentorship relationships, we do not merely shape the futures of those we serve - we forge the very foundations upon which the next generation of leaders, innovators, and changemakers will rise.

Living Your Best Life

Amidst the cacophony of modern life, the pursuit of a truly fulfilling existence can feel like a quest mired in the mists of ambiguity. Yet, embedded within the human experience lies a blueprint for Living Your Best Life - a roadmap forged from the hard-won lessons of those who have walked the path before us, luminaries whose legacies have cast an indelible glow upon the tapestry of human achievement.

To embark upon this transformative journey, we must first cultivate a profound sense of self-awareness - a clear-eyed understanding of our deepest values, our most cherished aspirations, and the unique contours of our individual narratives. For it is only by excavating the wellsprings of our authentic selves that we can begin to discern the bespoke path that will lead us to the realization of our fullest potential.

Through the practice of introspection, we unlock the doors to self-discovery, peeling back the layers of our subconscious to uncover the hidden truths that have long lain dormant within. Whether it's the unearthing of a long-suppressed creative passion, the recognition of an innate talent yearning to be nurtured, or the crystallization of a spiritual calling that resonates with the very core of our being, this process of self-examination lays the foundation upon which the edifice of our best lives can be constructed.

Armed with this clarity of vision, we are then empowered to translate our aspirations into tangible, actionable steps, imbuing our growth with a sense of momentum and purpose. Through the strategic deployment of goal-setting, the cultivation of unwavering discipline, and the judicious allocation of our time and resources, we position ourselves to transform the abstract into the achievable, chipping away at the barriers that have long stood between us and the realization of our dreams.

www.ingramcontent.com/pod-product-compliance
Lightning Source LLC
Chambersburg PA
CBHW071336130726
47996CB00002B/768